Jennifer LeClaire has made a tremendous contribution to the Body of Christ by exposing in detail the spirit of witchcraft and how to protect yourself against it. With key prophetic insight and practical tools, she boldly addresses the pitfalls and traps that have become so rampant in prophetic ministry. If you are ready to walk in a level of purity and freedom that you have never experienced before, I highly recommend this book.

—JEREMIAH JOHNSON
Best-selling author of *Trump and the Future of America*,
*The Power of Consecration*, and *Cleansing and Igniting the Prophetic*
Founder of Heart of the Father Ministry

# DISCERNING PROPHETIC WITCHCRAFT

DESTINY IMAGE BOOKS BY JENNIFER LECLAIRE

*The Spiritual Warrior's Guide to Defeating Water Spirits*

*Victory Decrees*

*The Seer Dimensions*

# DISCERNING PROPHETIC WITCHCRAFT

## EXPOSING THE SUPERNATURAL DIVINATION THAT IS DECEIVING SPIRITUALLY HUNGRY BELIEVERS

### JENNIFER LECLAIRE

DESTINY IMAGE® PUBLISHERS, INC.

P.O. Box 310, Shippensburg, PA 17257-0310

*"Promoting Inspired Lives."*

This book and all other Destiny Image and Destiny Image Fiction books are available at Christian bookstores and distributors worldwide.

Cover design by Eileen Rockwell
Interior design by Terry Clifton

For more information on foreign distributors, call 717-532-3040.

Reach us on the Internet: www.destinyimage.com.

ISBN 13 TP: 978-0-7684-5601-1
ISBN 13 eBook: 978-0-7684-5612-7
ISBN 13 HC: 978-0-7684-5614-1
ISBN 13 LP: 978-0-7684-5613-4

For Worldwide Distribution, Printed in the U.S.A.

3 4 5 6 7 8 / 24 23 22 21 20

# DEDICATION

This book is dedicated to every prophet—past, present and future—who refuses to bow a knee to Baal or kiss his mouth (see 1 Kings 19:18). While many false prophets are praised and their pockets overflow from merchandising unsuspecting saints, there is persecution against true prophets whose greatest desire is to speak forth the word of the Lord and equip the saints to hear His voice for themselves. We shouldn't be surprised. Jesus said it would be so. (See Luke 6:26 and Matthew 5:11.) I pray God will give you the grace to stand and withstand against the onslaught of prophetic witchcraft in the coming days and serve as a role model for the true prophetic. Like Paul the apostle, I ask you: "And pray for me, too. Ask God to give me the right words so I can boldly explain God's mysterious plan that the Good News is for Jews and Gentiles alike."

# ACKNOWLEDGMENTS

First, I want to thank Larry Sparks, publisher of Destiny Image and my dear friend, for suggesting I write this book. I have been writing about prophetic witchcraft, Jezebel, and false prophets for decades and, somehow, it did not occur to me to put my thoughts down in a greater work. Thanks, Larry, for discerning the critical need for this book in the times and seasons we find ourselves in. I am so very grateful to Christian International for setting a pure standard in the prophetic movement and refusing to compromise. I'm grateful for Bishop Bill Hamon, Tom and Jane, and the many others there who hold the plumb line.

# CONTENTS

# INTRODUCTION

Jennifer LeClaire has taken up the challenge of dealing with the false in the Church. The Bible talks about false apostles, prophets, teachers, and even false christs. It takes great wisdom to deal with a certain false thing in the Church without causing the reader to develop a fear of the true. Especially if the reader lacks the knowledge and experience in the true prophet movement, after reading about the problems a person could develop a fear of getting involved in the prophetic. This is especially true in dealing with the subject of false prophets and prophecy. An example of this was a book published by a charismatic publisher about ten years ago. The author wrote of sixteen atrocities in the prophet and prophetic ministry. The book was supposed to bring balance in the prophetic movement, but it only put fear in people concerning getting involved in any prophetic ministry. We at Christian International had two people who were enrolled to come to our prophetic training seminar cancel after reading that book.

Be assured that this is not the author's intent or desire, but rather to educate the saints so that they are not deceived and taken advantage of by these false ministers and ministries.

Because this subject is so important and delicate, I took time to read the whole book word for word to make sure Jennifer handled all these issues with wisdom and balance, to make sure everyone who reads this book still wants to get more involved in the prophetic ministry and God's prophets, who are preparing the way and making ready a people for the return of Christ Jesus.

Jennifer LeClaire, like Jeremiah, has felt the burden and commission from the Lord to reveal some of the unscriptural and false things that have infiltrated the prophetic movement. You need to know that Jennifer has been a leader in the prophetic movement for more than two decades. Just as I have, she has a passionate desire to see that the prophetic movement remains pure in doctrine and ministry with everything done in righteousness. We have a 100 percent passion for God's true prophets and prophetic ministry and a 100 percent passion to expose and eradicate the false prophets and wrongly motivated prophecies that manipulate people to fulfill the selfish desires of the prophet.

Most of the false teachings discussed in this book did not originate in the prophetic movement. They originally came out of the restoration movements that have happened over the last 500 years. But present-day ministers in the prophetic movement who do not have a thorough knowledge of church restoration movements think their new teaching is a revelation from God, but the deceiver has enlightened them with a false teaching and manifestations the same way he deceived the ministers who originated the false teaching. For instance, the false doctrine of universalism that is mentioned in this book, which teaches that all humans including satan and his fallen angels will be restored and make it into heaven. It was preached for the first time in 1500 and 1600 by a minister who came out of the Protestant movement. The same is true of the erroneous teaching of Preterism.

The extreme grace teaching, which allows Christians to live like the world and still be a Christian, was taught by erroneous teachers in the Latter Rain Movement of the 1950s. I was exposed to most of these false doctrines and manifestations. That's one reason I wrote the book called *How Can These Things Be?* I cover about fifteen false teachings and practices that have developed in the church world. Several of these false things have worked their way into the prophetic movement. In my trilogy of books on prophets and prophetic ministry, I reveal that there are many more true prophets than false in the 21st-century Church.

I am a church historian and have written more on Church restoration than any other Christian author in my book on Church restoration called *The Eternal Church*. It covers the eight movements God used to establish the Church in the First Reformation; the things that caused the deterioration of the Church into the Dark Age; the nine major restoration movements that restored all New Testament truths and ministries back into the Church during the Second Reformation; and the many things that will happen in the Third Reformation that will finalize all things for the second coming of Christ Jesus. The prophetic-apostolic movement fulfilled ten major truths and ministries that were not in the past restoration movements. Sad to say, like in every past restoration movement, satan seeks to infiltrate the movement with his false ministers and perverted ways of fulfilling the ministries.

Jennifer gives a good description of a person who could be called a false prophet. However, there are other categories of prophets who have a true heart but are questionable in their methods, prophecies, and motives. There are immature prophets, presumptuous prophets, and those who have a wrong concept of how prophets are to function and what they are to prophesy. I have been involved in prophetic ministry for 67 years. During the last 40 years we have trained hundreds who are called to be prophets, thousands of five-fold ministers to be prophetic ministers, and now more than 500,000 prophetic Christians around the world.

I am very jealous for God's prophets and the biblical ministry of the prophetic. It is the only ministry that the Bible tells God's people to covet: "covet to prophesy" (1 Cor. 14:39 KJV). "Pursue love, and desire spiritual gifts, but especially that you may prophesy" (1 Cor. 14:1). He who prophesies exhorts, edifies, comforts, and builds up the church (see 1 Cor. 14:4-5). "Brethren, desire earnestly to prophesy, and do not forbid to speak with tongues" (1 Cor. 14:39). "For you can all prophesy" (1 Cor. 14:31).

I received the commission to pioneer the prophetic movement when it was birthed in our second International Gathering of Prophets conference in 1988. I have been moving in prophetic ministry since I was 18 years old, and I am 85 now and still deeply involved in prophetic ministry. I wrote three books on the prophetic and prophets to introduce to the church world and to give guidelines: *Prophets and Personal Prophecy*, *Prophets and Prophetic Movement*, and *Prophets: Principles to Practice and Pitfalls to Avoid*. We started conducting prophetic seminars in 1983 and then in 1985 I developed a 300-page teaching manual on prophetic ministry. In the 1990s when the apostles were restored, I wrote the book, *Apostle-Prophets and the Coming Moves of God*. Over the last 35 years we have trained more than one-half million Christians in prophetic ministry.

If you are one of the few who may think this book is too strong against the abusers of the prophetic ministry, then I suggest you read prophet Jeremiah's book to the nation of Israel.

Bless you, Jennifer, for being willing to cover such a controversial subject, but after thoroughly reading the book and examining it closely, I consider you have done a thorough presentation. You have contrasted the true prophets and prophetic ministers to the false by using many scriptural proofs and wisdom gained from life experiences. Jennifer LeClaire has a passion for all ministers to be righteous and minister with the right motive and attitude, especially those who are prophets. That is one reason I received her as one of my spiritual daughters to help her fulfill her destiny, be covered, accountable, protected, and preserved victoriously until the end as a prophet leader in God's great company of prophets.

God bless everyone who reads this book with the spirit of wisdom and revelation to understand the difference between the true prophets and the false, yet still be a prophetic voice for God during this decade of the prophet.

BISHOP BILL HAMON
Bishop: Christian International Apostolic-Global Network
Author: *The Eternal Church; Prophets and Personal Prophecy;*
*Prophets and the Prophetic Movement; Prophets; Pitfalls; and*
*Principles; Apostles/Prophets and the Coming Moves of God;*
*The Day of the Saints; Who Am I and Why Am I Here;*
*Prophetic Scriptures Yet to be Fulfilled (Third Reformation);*
*70 Reasons for Speaking in Tongues; Your Highest Calling;*
*How Can These Things Be?* and *God's Weapons of War*

# Introduction

’m passionate about prophetic ministry—pure prophetic ministry. The restoration of five-fold prophets has helped edify, comfort, exhort, correct, unite and mature the Body of Christ since the 1980s. I’ve literally seen God transform lives through prophetic ministry. Now, a new generation of prophets and prophetic people are rising—and it’s exciting.

With the rise of true prophets and seers, is it any surprise we’re seeing the simultaneous rise of false prophets and seers? If it is, it shouldn’t be. Jesus warned us about false prophets in Matthew 7:15: “Beware of false prophets, who come to you in sheep’s clothing, but inwardly they are ravenous wolves.”

*The Passion Translation* puts a new light on this oft-quoted verse: “Constantly be on your guard against phony prophets. They come disguised as lambs, appearing to be genuine, but on the inside they are like wild, ravenous wolves!” And *The Message* says, “Be wary of false preachers who smile a lot, dripping with practiced sincerity. Chances are they are out to rip you off some way or other.”

It's important from the get-go to define what a false prophet is. A false prophet is not one who misses it or one who makes poor judgment calls in ministry operations as they learn and grow. No, a false prophet, in the simplest terms, is one who sets out to deceive. The motive is to gain something to consume upon their own lusts outside the will of God, whether that's money, fame, or some other reward. They don't seek God for what they need, but rather they manipulate their way into what they want.

Jesus gave us a second warning about false prophets in the end times in Matthew 24:11: "Then many false prophets will rise up and deceive many." Notice the double use of the word *many*. It doesn't say "a few false prophets will rise up and deceive unbelievers." It doesn't say "many false prophets will rise up and deceive a few." It paints a picture of a vast number of false prophets deceiving a vast number of people. In fact, the Greek word for *many* in that verse is *polus*. HELPS Word-studies defines it as "many (high in number); multitudinous, plenteous, much, great in amount (extent)."[1]

Maybe you have never heard false prophetic utterance first-hand or witnessed the operation of a false seer—or maybe you just haven't discerned these false functions yet. Let me assure you, as one who has walked on the front lines of the prophetic movement for decades, false prophets and false seers are emerging rapidly with manipulative cunning. False prophets appear to the undiscerning eye to be genuine, but they are seeking to devour. They seem sincere, but they are sincerely wrong in motives. It's important to exercise discernment, to examine the fruit rather than being enamored with a spiritual gift, charisma, or a large following.

The deception about which Jesus and New Testament writers warned is happening now on a large scale. It's not only emanating from prophetic merchandisers on late-night Christian TV with money gimmicks and miracle products we quite easily recognize as a scam. This deception is more subtle in the 21ˢᵗ century. And with the restoration of seers, we're witnessing a less familiar expression of the prophetic—dreams, visions, heavenly encounters, out-of-body experiences and the like—that fewer understand how to judge.

In truth, we've had a lot more training on how to hear the voice of God and judge a prophecy than we've had on visual revelation like seeing in the spirit or dreaming dreams. That's why I've launched The School of the Seers (www.schoolofthespirit.tv) and The Company of Seers (www.ignitenow.org), as well as The Global Prophetic Center (www.globalpropheticcenter.com) to train the masses around the world who are seeking truth.

## A Telling Dream

Some months before I penned this book, I had a disturbing dream in which I unexpectedly found myself on the same conference banner as someone I knew, without a doubt and through personal experience, was a false seer. This "prophet" was a last-minute addition to the event or I would not have agreed to attend. (I am as careful who I share a platform with as I can be. I won't knowingly minister with false prophets—even in dreams.)

Because I was already on my way to the event and did not want to cancel on the host, I kept moving forward trusting the Lord to work it out. When I arrived at the hotel, I walked into a lobby that looked like a replica of a 1960s rural America motel with a modern twist. The hotel lobby was small and antiquated, yet the reservations desk had all the modern technology you'd expect to see behind the counter. When I arrived, the clerk seemed confused and overwhelmed. I knew something was wrong, but did not yet know the extent of it.

After settling in, I drove from the hotel to the venue, a massive auditorium. I took my seat on the front row in between my ministry director and the host of the event. Just then, the conference host asked me what I thought of the man on the banner (the false seer). When I paused, he began to recite troubling issue after troubling issue with the false prophet's booking and travel. At this point, he regretted inviting him. I remained silent, but attentive. The host then admitted people had warned him not to invite this "prophet" in, but he didn't listen because he had been mesmerized by the gift.

Next, the host showed me a printed copy of an e-mail the prophet had sent his office. I did not see the full text of the e-mail, but the messaging was more than a little troublesome. At that point, the host was pleading for my wisdom. He implored me to advise him what to do before the situation grew worse and brought a reproach upon his ministry. I continued to be slow to speak, waiting on the Lord. As it turned out, the host was off the hook—and so was I—because the false prophet didn't show up.

## Heeding the Warning

The surface level meaning of this dream is not difficult to interpret. Some conference hosts are inviting people in to speak because they are enamored with a gift, not knowing until it's too late—or perhaps never knowing—that they are helping a false prophet propagate witchcraft. Some conference hosts find out after it's too late and have to make tough decisions. Many make the wrong ones and, at best, are complicit in releasing a spirit of error over those who come to their conferences. At worst, their attendees walk away with empty pockets, false prophetic promises, and demonic impartations.

But beyond this surface-level interpretation, there are many symbols in this dream worth noting. Consider the old hotel with the new technology. I believe this speaks to old "false prophet" tricks in a new season. The devil doesn't really have any new tricks so he recycles the old ones in a new generation—and they are more subtle.

Ultimately, this prophetic dream is a warning to the Body of Christ to know those who labor among you (see 1 Thess. 5:12). Be careful not to invite someone to your church because they dazzled you on Facebook with their spiritual gift. Character matters. If you are a pastor or an event host, you are responsible for who you bring in to speak to the people. Don't be an avenue of deception distribution by not checking out your speakers. This is a lesson we should not ignore. If you've made a mistake, it's always better to stop while you can before making a bigger mistake.

As you read the pages of this book, it's important to remind yourself not to throw the prophetic baby out with with dirty bathwater. A relatively small percentage of those who call themselves prophets are false prophets. The problem is, they are loud, charismatic and convincing. And because there's not enough teaching on what true prophets look like or how false prophets operate, many are being deceived.

## NOTE

1. HELPS Word-studies, s.v. "polus," https://biblehub.com/greek/4183.htm.

# CHAPTER 1

# TRUE PROPHECY IN THE 21ST CENTURY

Modern-day prophets are alive and well. They may not look like John the Baptist—complete with camel hair wardrobe and a shaggy beard—but the same Holy Spirit who moved prophets to speak bold words to kings, prophesy the end of famines, and raise the dead is walking the earth today. Indeed, tried and true, seasoned 21st century prophets are working tirelessly by the grace of God to fulfill the Ephesians 4:11 equipping mandate while simultaneously serving as heavenly minded mouthpieces of God.

Bishop Bill Hamon, widely known as the father of the modern-day prophetic movement, is still traveling the nations and equipping the saints for the work of the ministry well into his 80s (as of the time of this writing). Hamon, the founder of Christian International, has activated over half a million people in the prophetic and, perhaps just as important, has replicated replicators who are replicating replicators. In other words, he has raised up prophets who are raising up prophets who are raising up prophets—and so on.

"My revelation in 1983 was that God was going to raise up a company of prophets to 'prepare the way' and 'make ready a people' for the coming of the Lord Jesus as John the Baptist did for Christ's first coming," Hamon told me, calling it a fulfillment of Malachi 4:5-6:

> *See, I will send you Elijah the prophet before the coming of the great and dreaded day of the Lord. He will turn the hearts of the fathers to their children, and the hearts of the children to their fathers, lest I come and strike the earth with a curse* (MEV).

At the same time, emerging voices are rising with accuracy and boldness in what Hamon calls the "second wave" of the prophetic. The first wave of the prophetic was a restorative wave and an equipping and activation wave. That thrust won't stop, but Hamon says from this point forward prophets who go to the nations will not just prophesy information but release a word that causes nations to become either sheep nations or goat nations, depending on their response. Clearly, that's an end-times function that requires a great deal of authority and willingness to be persecuted.

"This is in preparation for Jesus, the Mighty Man of War, to come back and judge the nations according to Matthew 25:31 and Revelation 21:24," Hamon says. "We are commanded to prophesy again until resurrection life is activated. Don't wait. Prophesy to the issue you already heard the Lord on, and see yourself rise up along with the global Church as an exceeding great army" (see Ezek. 37:10).

# Global Prophetic Connections

I sit on the Apostolic Council of Prophetic Elders, originally launched by C. Peter Wagner and now headed by Cindy Jacobs, co-founder of Generals International. In 2017, based on a prophetic word from James Goll, she convened the first ever Global Prophetic Summit. Fifty-eight prophets from the nations of the earth gathered in Dallas to share what the Lord was saying and build cross-continental relationships. Some called it prophetic history in the making. I was there, and I would agree.

At that time, Hamon told me: "The lasting impact will be the fulfillment of God raising up and launching a company of prophets to fulfill His end-time purposes. I originally declared there would be hundreds of prophets in the USA and thousands throughout the world, not just a few here and there, but a company of prophets. It will be a sign and demonstration that we are in the second phase of the prophetic movement that was birthed in 1988."

Hamon says this is illustrated in Ezekiel 37—and 1988 until now has been the noising abroad of the message of the prophetic movement. As he sees it, it caused a shaking in the Church. The bones came together as different prophetic networks were formed, then books and teaching put muscle and sinew together and formed a body or company of prophets.

Those who have been walking in the prophetic movement for a decade or more understand firsthand the challenges we face in the movement Hamon launched. Perhaps the underlying challenge, Hamon told me, is raising up prophets who have their ten Ms—manhood, ministry, message, maturity, marriage, methods, manners, money, morality, and motives—in order and have more specific and accurate words for the Church and nations and God's timing for His purposes to be fulfilled.

Many are asking the question: How do we overcome the challenges we see in the prophetic movement? Hamon has some wisdom:

> Have more communication between prophets and church with each other before putting out a word that has national or world events. It's not enough to get a word; we need counsel and wisdom for presentation and some idea of the timing. We have seen words of world events or catastrophes to happen.
>
> In my 64 years [of ministry], I have heard many such prophecies but few have come to pass at that time. Like in the Old Testament, many prophecies took centuries before fulfillment. Such as Messianic prophecies and judgments to nations. Younger-arising prophets need to be trained and mentored like Elisha was by Elijah.

## Walking in the Prophetic Reset

Here's what I know: We stand at one of the greatest eras in the prophetic movement in the history of mankind. We are entering the prophetic reset and many positive developments are in the works. As part of this prophetic reset, we are going to see true prophetic ministries refocus on several key initiatives and prophetic people will respond in kind.

While companies of false prophets will try to mimic God's true mouthpieces, discerning hearts will clearly see the difference. Although false prophets will rise and deceive many, we must grow in discernment rather than shunning the vital work of prophets. Here's some of what the Lord showed me the prophetic reset looks like:

### True, Mature Prophets Will Equip the Saints

True, mature prophets will place a greater emphasis on equipping the saints. In recent years we've seen the rise of "conference prophets" who are not teaching or imparting anything more than a goose bump. Conferences can be strategic and even life-changing, but let's face it—sometimes it's just another conference. Without equipping, the saints will fall to the deception of false prophets. This is why I started my School of the Prophets in 2016 (www.schoolofthespirit.tv), which is now headquartered in two nations.

Indeed, God is reemphasizing the Ephesians 4 mandate in the prophetic movement. Equipping is the primary function of a New Testament prophet (who has matured enough to teach others). Of course, prophets are going to prophesy. That's a given. You don't have to wonder if a dog is going to bark. Of course, a dog is going to bark. But the primary function of the dog is not to bark. The primary function of the dog is to be a companion to man, or in some cases to hunt or to sniff out criminal activity. Barking is important, but it's not the dog's primary role. This is the Ephesians 4 mandate:

*And He Himself gave some to be apostles, some prophets, some evangelists, and some pastors and teachers, for the equipping of the saints for the work of ministry, for the edifying of the body of Christ, till we all come to the unity of the faith and of the knowledge of the Son of God, to a perfect man, to the measure of the stature of the fullness of Christ; that we should no longer be children, tossed to and fro and carried about with every wind of doctrine, by the trickery of men, in the cunning craftiness of deceitful plotting, but, speaking the truth in love, may grow up in all things into Him who is the head—Christ— from whom the whole body, joined and knit together by what every joint supplies, according to the effective working by which every part does its share, causes growth of the body for the edifying of itself in love* (Ephesians 4:11-16).

Ephesians 4:11 is a precursor to the Saints Movement. Hamon prophesied a Saints Movement in 2007:

The Saints Movement is a time when the saints, believers in Jesus Christ, recognize and act on the understanding that Christ has empowered and commissioned each of them to be the Church 24/7— manifesting the Kingdom of God wherever they live and work. Every believer has the ability to manifest the supernatural in a miraculous way, and every saint is called to demonstrate the Gospel of the Kingdom (not just the Gospel of salvation) in their sphere of influence.

The Saints Movement was birthed in 2007 and prepared the way of heaven's decree for the beginning of "The Third and Final Church Reformation" in 2008.

> Christ's Third Apostolic Reformation and purpose is to use His restored Church to fulfill God's original mandate to mankind—subdue all things, take dominion and fill the earth with a mankind race in God's own image and likeness, bring more and more of God's Kingdom and will to earth, and transform nations into sheep nations (those who do the works of Christ. See Matthew 25:31-46). This is the end result of the saints taking the Gospel of the Kingdom into every aspect of society.

### More Prophets Will Join Schools

Beyond prophets equipping believers, we're going to see true prophets entering continuing education themselves. We're in the second wave of the prophetic movement, yet many schools of the prophets are training the gift of prophecy instead of the office of the prophet. The result is prophets who are strong in prophecy but, at times, ill-equipped to walk in the stature, diplomacy, and character the office requires.

Of course, training prophets is not a new idea. Samuel had a school of the prophets (see 1 Sam. 19). Second Kings 2 points to Elijah's school of the prophets. And Second Kings 4 points to Elisha's school of the prophets. We still need to train the gift—believers need to be activated and trained to function prophetically—but part of the prophetic reset is a greater emphasis on training those in the office than we've seen in the past—and not just how to prophesy, but Christology, prophetology, integrity, and the like.

### *Emphasis on Commissioning*

As part of the prophetic reset, we're going to see more strategic commissioning as opposed to mail-order ordinations. The actual definition of *commission* is "granting the power to perform various acts or duties," "a certificate conferring military rank and authority," or "a charge," according to *Merriam-Webster*'s dictionary.[1] More elders in the prophetic will be moved by the Holy Spirit to intentionally train and commission younger prophets like Elijah commissioned Elisha.

The second wave prophet's commissioning will be relational, not online-network-only-based where you can join a network for a monthly fee without any relationship whatsoever. Strategic commissioning is more than filling out an application and receiving a certificate from someone you don't really know and who doesn't really know you. Some won't like these relational requirements because we live in a microwave generation where people want everything now without much investment, but the sons of the prophets will arise seeking mothers and fathers in the faith.

Emerging prophets need to be taught there is a space of time between the calling and the commissioning and that without relationship there is no safety net. When Paul commissioned his spiritual son Timothy, there was relationship, accountability, and a charge: "This charge I commit to you, son Timothy, according to the prophecies previously made concerning you, that by them you may wage the good warfare" (1 Tim. 1:18). I'm looking for Elishas—prophets, seers, watchman, warriors, and intercessors—to pass my mantle to. I want to commission prophets through the Global Prophetic Center (globalpropheticcenter.com) and pour into young lives through the Elisha internship at Awakening House of Prayer.

### Greater Emphasis on Seer Gift

As part of the prophetic reset, we're seeing a greater emphasis on the seer gift. We've spent much of the prophetic movement focused on hearing the voice of the Lord. We've had some emphasis on dreams, which is part of the seer dimensions. (You can pick up a copy of my book *The Seer Dimensions* to learn more.) But visions are less understood, as are out-of-body experiences, spirit travel, and other types of biblical encounters.

Joel prophesied, "And it shall come to pass afterward that I will pour out My Spirit on all flesh; your sons and your daughters shall prophesy, your old men shall dream dreams, your young men shall see visions" (Joel 2:28). God is opening up visions, many types of visions, to His people. We need to be like Jesus and seek to see what the Father is doing so we can get in line with His will. Indeed, we are in a new era of seers. I've been teaching on the seer anointing in my School of the Seers since 2018, have raised up a Company of Seers through the Ignite network, and have written several books on the seer anointing, including *The Seer Dimensions*.

### Companies of Prophets Rising

More prophets are gathering in companies, hubs, and nests. In 2015, I co-authored a book called *Revival Hubs Rising: Revealing a New Ministry Paradigm for the Next Great Move of God*. The book highlights how houses of prayer, revival hubs, apostolic centers, prophetic nets, and the like would begin to rise. We've seen that and will see more of it in the years ahead. Indeed, we're going to see many prophetic hubs rise with leaders who have a gathering anointing to attract prophets with mighty calls who have been walking alone for far too long.

As the restoration of the Tabernacle of David continues—that is, as the global prayer and worship movement continues rising—we will see Davidic prophets rise. These Davidic prophets will be worshiping, warring prophets with a leadership mantle to gather prophetic outcasts who have been shunned, shamed, and shifted out of mainstream churches. Some of them will be like David's mighty men in First Samuel 22:2: *"Everyone in distress or in debt or discontented gathered to him, and he became a commander over them"* (AMPC).

Even now, I hear the Lord saying, "Even though walking as a prophet can be lonely at times, I have not called my prophets to walk alone. I have called you to submit yourselves one to another, to stir one another up, to encourage each other in the face of growing persecution and to war with and for each other in the dark days." Through my Ignite Network, we have established Lighthouses where companies of prophets and prophetic people can gather together and do prophetic life together.

### *Beware the Obadiah Phenomenon*

As these companies, nests, and hubs arise, we have to be careful about the Obadiah phenomenon. We find the Obadiah phenomenon in First Kings 18:4: "For so it was, while Jezebel massacred the prophets of the Lord, that Obadiah had taken one hundred prophets and hidden them, fifty to a cave, and had fed them with bread and water."

What does the Obadiah phenomenon look like in the modern-day prophetic movement? There are a few issues we must watch. First, it looks like prophets who hide in their own companies, never venturing out of their nest to synergize with prophets who have different expressions than their own. We see this even now, with prophets entrenched in specific camps—the doom and gloom camp, the grace camp, the glory camp, etc.— and it's not healthy.

The First Kings companies of prophets were isolated in two companies—and they were isolated from every other prophet in Israel. Even between the two companies in close-by caves, there was no intermingling. There was no connection or community. They couldn't pray together, worship together, share their prophetic words with one another. Their perspectives grew limited without any fresh revelation from prophets outside their own camp.

God is working to break down silos in the prophetic so we can truly work together. It's fine and good to have your own company, but when we deny the power of other expressions we're shutting out revelation that could add to our own view. Remember, we know in part and we prophesy in part (see 1 Cor. 13:9). We need all the parts to come together—all the bones to come together. Many streams make a great river.

Remember, Obadiah took 100 prophets and split them down the middle. Prophets—the voice of God—should not be divided. Although God is surely saying many things to many prophets at once, the Holy Spirit does not speak with a forked tongue. It's difficult for the Body of Christ to know what prophet to follow when there is so much contradiction. Part of the problem, as Hamon pointed out, is a lack of communication. Hubs, companies, and nests—along with cross-pollination among prophetic camps—help solve that issue.

### Prophets Will Not Hide from Jezebel

In the past, many prophets ran from Jezebel, a seducing spirit that leads people into immorality and idolatry (see Rev. 2:20). Even Elijah, who confronted the false prophets who ate at Jezebel's table, ran from Jezebel. Consider Elijah's mistake. After defeating the false prophets at the showdown at Mount Carmel, he succumbed to Jezebel's witchcraft (see 2 Kings 9:22).

> Ahab told Jezebel all that Elijah had done, also how he had executed all the prophets with the sword. Then Jezebel sent a messenger to Elijah, saying, "So let the gods do to me, and more also, if I do not make your life as the life of one of them by tomorrow about this time." And when he saw that, he arose and ran for his life, and went to Beersheba, which belongs to Judah, and left his servant there.
>
> But he himself went a day's journey into the wilderness, and came and sat down under a broom tree. And he prayed that he might die, and said, "It is enough! Now, Lord, take my life, for I am no better than my fathers!"
>
> Then as he lay and slept under a broom tree, suddenly an angel touched him, and said to him, "Arise and eat." Then he looked, and there by his head was a cake baked on coals, and a jar of water. So he ate and drank, and lay down again. And the angel of the Lord came back the second time, and touched him, and said, "Arise and eat, because the journey is too great for you." So he arose, and

*ate and drank; and he went in the strength of that food forty days and forty nights as far as Horeb, the mountain of God* (1 Kings 19:1-8).

Elijah later anointed Jehu, whose assignment was to take Jezebel down. I believe Elijah missed it partly because he did not have the support of other prophets. He didn't have a company of prophets to pray for him when Jezebel's witchcraft attacked his mind. In fact, Elijah left his servant behind, the only one who could have talked some sense into him. Elijah needed a prophetic hub to run to like the apostles had in the Book of Acts. When the Pharisees beat and threatened James and John after the man at the Gate Beautiful was healed, the Bible says they ran back to their own company for prayer (see Acts 4:23).

### God Is Calling Prophets Out of the Cave

God is calling prophets out of the cave. God is dealing with prophets who are hiding from the persecution of Jezebel and religion, which is part of the Obadiah phenomenon. The Hebrew word for *hide* in First Kings 18:4 means withdrawal. Prophets can't withdraw from society. Prophets should speak into society. We are in the world but not of the world. We are not hermits. We need to know what is going on in the world. When a major event breaks out in the earth, we should have a prophetic opinion.

As I said in the beginning of this chapter, modern-day prophets are alive and well. We must not throw out the prophetic ministry altogether just because prophetic witchcraft has infiltrated some camps or because false prophets are rising, as Jesus said they would. Rather, we must hold fast to the truth and embrace the ministry of true prophets who are committed to delivering the unadulterated prophetic word of God and equipping believers to discern God's voice, know His will, and see what the Father is doing.

## NOTE

1. Merriam-Webster, s.v. "commission," https://www.merriam-webster.com/dictionary/commission.

# CHAPTER 2

# WHAT A REAL PROPHET LOOKS LIKE

What do real prophets look like? Well, let's start with the advice from Jesus, our Prototype Prophet. Jesus said you would know prophets by their fruit (see Matt. 7:16). You could also say it this way: You will know them by the effect of their prophetic functions, the spirit behind their utterance, and the consistency of their character. You can also discern a true prophet by the frequency, accuracy, and weight of the words they release.

Although Old and New Testament prophets share some similar functions, for example, the New Testament prophet is operating out of a different covenant. Old Testament prophets operated under the Law and prophesied the coming of Christ. New Testament prophets are prophesying the Second Coming, the restoration of all things, in a dispensation of grace. So the baseline difference is one of the era we live in. Under the Law, prophets who missed it were stoned. Under the new covenant, there is room for fallibility among prophets who are sincere in their utterance.

While some well-meaning people have created Internet checklists telling us what a prophet looks like, the best way to discover how true prophets function, utter, and otherwise walk worthy of their calling is to study the lives of prophets displayed in the pages of the Bible itself. I call this prophetology—the study of prophets. God has set forth a certain standard for prophets. Prophets weep over things most people don't notice. Prophets get angry over injustices to which many turn a blind eye—or don't even discern. Prophets carry a burden for things that burden God. Prophets hate what God hates and love what God loves at a deep level.

Prophets see in black and white. Prophets are intercessors. Prophets stand for God in the world. Prophets become signs. Prophets create spiritual atmospheres where the Holy Spirit feels welcome. Prophets deal with sin. Prophets can be dramatic at times. Prophets speak boldly against societal evils and idolatry. Prophets contend with false authority. Prophets prophesy. Prophets are friends of God. Prophets think outside the box. Prophets are supernatural. Prophets are dreamers. Prophets are persecuted.

Some years ago while ministering in Singapore, I was sitting at a lunch table with David Ravenhill, the son of the late and great revivalist Leonard Ravenhill. We were with a group of leaders, some megachurch pastors and some intercessors, who were giving sincere thanks for my coming to the nation and imparting and equipping in the realm of prayer.

After a few minutes of this, Ravenhill jokingly quoted Jesus in Luke 6:26: "Woe to you when all men speak well of you, for so did their fathers to the false prophets." We all laughed, but he made a good point. Prophets in the Bible weren't treated like celebrities—and often weren't celebrated at all. In fact, Elijah, Jeremiah, and others weren't typically well-received. Rather, some prophets of old were often murdered because of their message. Isaiah was sawed in half. Jeremiah was stoned to death. John the Baptist was beheaded. Jesus told the Pharisees:

> *Woe to you, scribes and Pharisees, hypocrites! Because you build the tombs of the prophets and adorn the monuments of the righteous, and say, "If we had lived in the days of our fathers, we would not have been partakers with them in the blood of the prophets." Therefore you are witnesses against yourselves that you are sons of those who murdered the prophets* (Matthew 23:29-31).

My point is, you can't discern a true prophet based on the size of their Facebook following cheering them on almost to the point of deification, the number of people who show up to their meetings, the type of car they drive, the quality of clothes they wear, or anything that can be measured by the world's standards. Again, you judge a true prophet by the fruit of their function, utterance, and character.

## Functions of the Modern-Day Prophet

The New Testament prophet is not called to function as a mirror image of Old Testament prophets. We have a better covenant based on better promises (see Heb. 8:6). God didn't change—God never changes—but the covenant changed and with the New Covenant the purpose for prophets progressed. For example, Old Testament prophets had two overarching functions: to foretell the coming of Christ in the flesh and to warn Israelites about coming judgment for breaking the Ten Commandments.

In the New Testament, the primary purpose of the prophet is found in Ephesians 4:11-16:

> *And He Himself gave some to be apostles, some prophets, some evangelists, and some pastors and teachers, for the equipping of the saints for the work of ministry, for the edifying of the body of Christ, till we all come to the unity of the faith and of the knowledge of the Son of God, to a perfect man, to the measure of the stature of the fullness of Christ; that we should no longer be children, tossed to and fro and carried about with every wind of doctrine, by the trickery of men, in the cunning craftiness of deceitful plotting, but, speaking the truth in love, may grow up in all things into Him who is the head—Christ—from whom the whole body, joined and knit together by what every joint supplies, according to the effective working by which every part does its share, causes growth of the body for the edifying of itself in love.*

If more prophets were fulfilling this primary function, we would see fewer false prophets deceiving the saints. Prophets with the heart of God understand they have a part to play in maturing the Body of Christ by teaching people how to hear the voice of God for themselves, bringing unity to the Body of Christ by sharing the mind and will of God, helping the Bride avoid the deception of the wicked one who works to plant weeds in the field of our mind, and so on.

Of course, New Testament prophets will prophesy and deliver true rebukes of the Spirit, directional words, and other utterances that go beyond the simple gift of prophecy. But if we look at Jesus, the Prototype Prophet, we'll see that although He worked miracles, raised the dead, cast out devils, operated in the gifts of the Spirit and more, He was intentional about equipping His disciples to do the same. Jesus didn't just preach at large outdoor open meetings, He also taught. He discipled. He corrected.

In some ways, a prophet is still a prophet no matter what chapter and verse you read in the Bible. In other words, there are common functions of prophets, who are mouthpieces for God. Although true prophets have an equipping mandate, that is not their only mandate. While equipping is the primary focus of the New Testament prophet, there are many Old Testament functions of the prophet that rolled over into the new covenant.

Prophets make announcements. Prophets bring confirmation. Prophets guard the vision. Prophets judge prophecy. Prophets pull down, destroy, and throw down. Prophets build and plant. Prophets correct. Prophets rebuke. Prophets encourage. Prophets are futurists. Prophets bring direction. Prophets warn. Prophets interpret dreams and visions and much more. There are many different types of prophets, from worshiping prophets, to scribing prophets, to healing prophets, to seer prophets, to preaching prophets and beyond.

### Standing in the Gap

Have you considered the priesthood of the prophetic? The Bible says we are priests and kings (see 1 Pet. 2:9). A priest in the common sense of the word is one who is authorized to act as an intermediary between man and God. We know that Jesus is our mediator and we need no other (see 1 Tim. 2:5). Nevertheless, God has chosen not to do anything in the earth unless someone in this realm makes a petition. In other words, God won't work unless we pray.

The Lord said, "I sought for a man among them, that should make up the hedge, and stand in the gap before me for the land, that I should not destroy it: but I found none" (Ezek. 22:30 KJV). All prophets are intercessors. People argue with me about that, but my thought is this: If you don't pray, you don't have anything to say. I don't want a prophetic word from someone who is not a prayerful person. The Bible backs me up on this thought.

Jeremiah 27:18 tells us, "But if they are prophets, and if the word of the Lord is with them, let them now make intercession to the Lord of hosts, that the vessels which are left in the house of the Lord, in the house of the king of Judah, and at Jerusalem, do not go to Babylon." The New Living Translation puts the first half of that verse this way: "If they really are prophets and speak the Lord's messages, let them pray to the Lord of Heaven's Armies."

Every now and again, I put up a post on Facebook that says, "All prophets are intercessors but not all intercessors are prophets." That seems to make some people angry. They argue that they don't have to pray or intercede. Every believer is called to intercede according to First Timothy 2:1: "Therefore I exhort first of all that supplications, prayers, intercessions, and giving of thanks be made for all men."

How much more those who are speaking for the Lord God Almighty? Prayer is conversation with God. Every prophetic word doesn't come out of the place of intercession, but if you set your heart toward intercession you will surely receive instruction. You are digging a well. You are building relationship with God, renewing your mind, learning His ways. In prayer, if you speak as a prophet about a situation that concerns Him, He will likely speak back. Amos 3:7 reveals, "Surely the Lord God does nothing, unless He reveals His secret to His servants the prophets."

Consider this: The very first time you ever see the word *prophet* in the Bible, it is connected to prayer. In the Book of Genesis when Abimelech took Abraham's wife in innocence, the Lord said, "Now therefore, restore the man's wife; for he is a prophet, and he will pray for you and you shall live. But if you do not restore her, know that you shall surely die, you and all who are yours" (Gen. 20:7). Old Testament or New, you can't separate the prophet from prayer. It is the lifeblood of the prophetic because it is our connection with God and His will.

### Turning Hearts to the Father

False prophets turn the hearts of God's people to themselves. True prophets turn the hearts of people back to our heavenly Father—they point people to Jesus. Malachi 4:5-6 shares God's heart in this matter:

> *Behold, I will send you Elijah the prophet before the coming of the great and dreadful day of the Lord. And he will turn the hearts of the fathers to the children, and the hearts of the children to their fathers, lest I come and strike the earth with a curse.*

We know Elijah turned the heart of Israel back to God at the showdown of Mount Carmel. One prophetic word can turn a stony heart to flesh that seeks God again. But this also relates to repentance. True prophets don't tickle ears. They encourage when God wants to encourage, direct when God wants to direct, but call for repentance when God is grieved by behaviors. The late revivalist Leonard Ravenhill once said, "A popular evangelist reaches your emotions. A true prophet reaches your conscience." Selah.

## *The Spirit of a Reformer*

Old Testament or New, the spirit of reformation charges prophetic ministry. The prophetic ministry is called to bring change—positive change. This reforming spirit brought hope to the people. Elijah is a prime example. He challenged the people to declare whom they would serve—Jehovah or Baal. His reformation message sought to turn the hearts of men away from pagan gods.

What about the Prophet Haggai? Haggai's reforming message challenged Israel to rebuild God's temple so they could receive His blessings. Don't forget the prophetess Deborah. She united the Israelites against the Canaanites during a time no men were willing to lead. She led her nation in victory, bringing freedom to Israel.

The Old Testament is filled with prophetic reformers. Ezekiel, Jeremiah, Isaiah, Malachi. It's a common characteristic that accompanies the prophetic anointing in any era. Moving into the New Testament, we see John the Baptist with his reformation message and, of course, Jesus, the mighty Reformer, who came to reform religion as His day knew it. You can't divide a reformation mindset from the prophetic. Prophets have reformation in their DNA.

The prophet's goal is to see God's best for people and nations and they take action to bring change, whether that is in the heart of man, in spiritual warfare, or in building efforts of some sort. The apostles, remember, aren't the only five-fold ascension gift called to build. The prophetic ministry builds and plants. The apostle and prophet build in different ways, but their desire is the same—to see the glorious Church without spot or wrinkle filled with equipped, triumphant saints.

## Preparing a People for the Lord

Prophets are called to prepare a way for the Lord and to prepare people for the Lord. John the Baptist, a transitional prophet being the last of the Old Testament prophets and the first of the New Testament prophets, was called to prepare a way for the Lord, to make His paths straight (see Matt. 3:2-4). He was a messenger and this was his message: "Repent!"

John the Baptist carried the spirit of Elijah that Malachi discussed. The Bible says John was filled with the Holy Ghost, even from his mother's womb (see Luke 1:15). An angel of the Lord told Zacharias, John's father, what to expect before the child was ever conceived: "He will also go before Him in the spirit and power of Elijah, 'to turn the hearts of the fathers to the children,' and the disobedient to the wisdom of the just, to make ready a people prepared for the Lord" (Luke 1:17).

So we see the angel of the Lord prophesied that John would come in the spirit and power of Elijah to turn the hearts of the fathers toward the children and the hearts of the children back to the will of God. Preparing a people for the Lord, then, is preparing their spirit and their souls—their spirits to receive wisdom and revelation in the knowledge of Him and their soul to align with the Spirit.

## *Separating the Profane from the Holy*

Prophets in the Old and New Testament alike separate the profane from the holy. The Lord tells us to be holy even as He is holy (see 1 Pet. 1:16). To be holy is to be devoted entirely to God and His work, to be consecrated for His purposes.

The word *profane* simply means unsanctified, secular, or irreverent. It doesn't take a prophet to discern the difference, yet it does take a prophetic anointing to separate the holy from the profane when the two have grown up together. This is part of the prophetic anointing to root out (see Jer. 1) and may require deliverance ministry.

But that's just one way to separate the holy from the profane. The second way prevents demonic strongholds in the first place by calling a sin a sin before the devil takes up residence in the believer's soul. Prophets carry a grace that convicts people of their sin. We know that Jonah went to Nineveh with a message of repentance. The people believed God, proclaimed a fast, and put on sackcloth, from the greatest of them even to the least of them (see Jonah 3). We know that the Lord told Isaiah to "cry aloud...lift up thy voice like a trumpet, and shew my people their transgression" (Isa. 58:1 KJV). And we know that the Lord told Ezekiel to *"cause Jerusalem to know her abominations"* (Ezek. 16:1-2).

This is an area where Old Testament and New Testament operations intersect, for the apostle Paul wrote in his first epistle to the church at Corinth about the grace of the prophetic to convict of sin. Read this truth in First Corinthians 14:24-25:

> *But if all prophesy [giving inspired testimony and interpreting the divine will and purpose] and an unbeliever*

*or untaught outsider comes in, he is told of his sin and reproved and convicted and convinced by all, and his defects and needs are examined (estimated, determined) and he is called to account by all, the secrets of his heart are laid bare; and so, falling on [his] face, he will worship God, declaring that God is among you in very truth* (AMPC).

This doesn't just apply to unbelievers, but also Christians. When I was young in the Lord there was an elder prophet in our church. She would preach now and then when the apostle was traveling. When people heard she was going to preach, the word got out that, "You better start repenting now." That's because her messages, though not condemning, always seemed to bring conviction to our hearts. She was a true prophet, separating the profane from the holy with purity.

## Prophetic Functions

Of course, there are many other aspects of prophetic ministry. Spiritual warfare, deliverance, understanding times and seasons, making decrees and announcements, encouraging the weak, being a watchman and issuing warnings, imparting spiritual gifts, confirming and activating, and foretelling and forthtelling.

Indeed, there are many aspects to the prophetic ministry, and yet no two prophets are alike. God uses some prophets more in the area of foretelling and forthtelling. He uses others more in the area of warnings. He uses some more in the area of deliverance. Just like no two Christians are alike, no two prophets are alike. However, all prophets should have the same heartbeat—the heartbeat John the beloved heard when he laid his head on Jesus' chest (see John 13:23). The foundation of prophetic ministry should be built on standing in the gap with intercessions, turning hearts to God, preparing a people to know and do His will, and separating the profane from the holy.

We must align ourselves with the heart of the prophetic under the order of Melchizedek so that all that flows from it is based on right motivations (see Heb. 5:10). New Testament prophets aren't functioning after the order of Aaron, the Levite. They are functioning under the same order as Jesus, the order of Melchizedek. It's the prophets who aren't flowing in that order who are hijacking the prophetic ministry.

## Understanding the Ten Ms

Bishop Hamon developed what he calls the ten "M" guidelines for ministers. These apply equally to prophets and were written in the context of Hamon's books on prophetic ministry.

The first M is manhood. Hamon points to Genesis 1:26-27 and asserts God makes a man before manifesting his ministry. Jesus walked the earth for 30 years before He started His public ministry—a ministry that ultimately only lasted three and half years on the earth. That's a ten to one ratio in preparation time versus ministry time.

Hamon implores us to look at the man (or woman) apart from the title, position, message, or ministry. Has the man been conformed to the image of Christ (see Rom. 8:29)? We are all in process. There is a making process for prophets, which I wrote about in my book *The Making of a Prophet.* God can surely use a young, unprocessed person to prophesy, but promotion that comes too quick often results in an anointing that character can't sustain—and ultimately a fall. Hamon urges us to look at the person and not just the performance.

The second M is ministry. Are they free from offense in ministry (see 2 Cor. 6:3)? Is there a demonstration of power (see 1 Cor. 2:4-5)? Does the anointing on their life produce godly results (see Matt. 7:15-21)? Is their prophecy and preaching productive, pure, and positive (see Deut. 18:12)?

The third M is message. Does the prophet speak the truth in love according to Ephesians 4:15? Is the message balanced, scriptural, doctrinally and spiritually right (see 1 Tim. 4:2)?

The fourth M is maturity. Do they have a right attitude; are they mature in human relations and demonstrating heavenly wisdom (see James 3:17)? Do they operate in the fruit of the Spirit, with Christlike character? Are they dependable and steadfast (see Gal. 5:22)? Are they biblically knowledgeable and not a novice?

The fifth M is marriage. If they are married, is their marriage scripturally in order—God, family, ministry (see 1 Tim. 3:2,5; 1 Pet. 3:1,7)? Does their marriage exemplify the relationship of Christ and His Church (see Eph. 4:22-23)?

The sixth M is methods. Are they rigidly righteous, ethical, honest, and integrity-upright (see Tit. 1:16)? Do they shun manipulation and deception (see Rom. 1:18)? Good end results do not justify unscriptural means (see Rom. 3:7-8).

The seventh M is manners. Are they unselfish, polite, kind, and discreet (see Tit. 1:7; 3:1-2)? Do they use proper speech and communication in words and mannerisms (see Eph. 4:29; 5:4)?

The eighth M is money. Are they craving wealth and resorting to ignoble and dishonest methods (see 1 Tim. 3:8 AMP)?

The ninth M is morality. Are they involved in virtuous, pure, and proper relationships (see 1 Cor. 6:9-18)? Are they adhering to biblical sexual purity in attitude and action (see Eph. 5:3)?

The tenth M is motive. Is their motive to serve or to be seen? To fulfill a personal drive or God's mission (see Matt. 6:1)? Are they motivated by God's love or lust for power, fame, and name?

You won't necessarily be able to answer all of these questions the first time you hear someone speak—but you may discern something is out of line. Some of these questions you may never have the answer to, but if you pay attention to the words coming out of the prophet's mouth, you'll eventually hear what's in their heart. Out of the abundance of the heart, the mouth speaks (see Luke 6:45).

You can also investigate to see who someone is aligned with, but even then false prophets have deceived true prophets so the most devious phony prophet could be aligned with a giant in the prophetic who was bewitched through flattery or divination. Alignments are important, but alignments are not the test of a true prophet. The bottom line is we should not be quick to align ourselves with anyone's ministry; we should be quick, rather, to discern the will of the Lord for the ministries we feed from and support.

# CHAPTER 3

# SIGNS OF FALSE PROPHETS

L ike the demons that inspire them, false prophets have been roaming about seeking to fleece unsuspecting sheep since Moses walked the earth—or at least God has been warning us about these pseudo ministers since then. As far back as the Book of Deuteronomy—the fifth book of the Bible—Jehovah started making mention of false prophets:

> *If there arises among you a prophet or a dreamer of dreams, and he gives you a sign or a wonder, and the sign or the wonder comes to pass, of which he spoke to you, saying, "Let us go after other gods"—which you have not known—"and let us serve them," you shall not listen to the words of that prophet or that dreamer of dreams, for the Lord your God is testing you to know whether you love the Lord your God with all your heart and with all your soul. You shall walk after the Lord your God and fear Him, and keep His commandments and obey His voice; you shall serve Him and hold fast to*

*Him. But that prophet or that dreamer of dreams shall be put to death, because he has spoken in order to turn you away from the Lord your God, who brought you out of the land of Egypt and redeemed you from the house of bondage, to entice you from the way in which the Lord your God commanded you to walk. So you shall put away the evil from your midst* (Deuteronomy 13:1-5).

Notice the first mention of a false prophet includes the operations of dreams, signs, and wonders. Of the many characteristics of false prophets we'll explore in this book, the baseline sign of a false prophet is found way back in Deuteronomy 13—they lead you away from God rather than to Him. False prophets are still leading people away from Jesus today. As a matter of fact, with the proliferation of true prophets, it seems false prophets have taken the opportunity to prey on people who are hungry to hear the voice of God at any cost (even willing to pay for prophetic words).

Yes, there are modern-day false prophets operating in counterfeit anointings. When Jesus walked the earth, He warned, "Beware of false prophets, who come to you in sheep's clothing, but inwardly they are ravenous wolves" (Matt. 7:15). No, they don't really come dressed as sheep, but they do prey like wolves, and if they do pray they usually pray witchcraft prayers. (Witchcraft prayers are prayers that are in line with their will rather than God's will.) Sadly, too many believers are falling for the false hope of false prophets and sowing into their coffers, thereby enabling them to continue their false ministries and deceive more desperate sheep.

Discernment is needed in the Body of Christ as many are enamored with accurate words of knowledge and breakthrough prophecies. We must test the spirits speaking. John the beloved wrote, "Dear friends, do not believe everyone who claims to speak by the Spirit. You must test them to see if the spirit they have comes from God. For there are many false prophets in the world" (1 John 4:1 NLT).

So what can we take away from this?

1.  There are many false prophets in the world.

2.  It's up to us to discern the true from the false.

3.  We have to judge prophecy.

The devil always makes a counterfeit of what's real. The New Testament makes reference to the term *false prophets* eleven times. Jesus talked about them. Peter talked about them. And John talked about them. The Old Testament mentions false prophets over and over again. Just as there are characteristics of true prophets, there are clear signs of false prophets. What you discover about these wolves in sheep's clothing may surprise you.

## Three Types of Prophets

The Bible highlights three kinds of prophets—the prophets of Baal, the prophets of Jezebel, and the prophets of Jehovah. Baal is a god of prophetic divination. This spirit leads people into idolatry today just like it led the Israelites into idolatry when Moses was up on the mountain. Remember how the children of Israel made a molten calf as an idol to worship in Exodus 32:8? That was the spirit of Baal inspiring the spiritual harlotry.

Modern-day prophets of Baal release prophetic utterances that aim to lead you to serve what you want instead of serving God

43

and God alone. In other words, they lead you away from God to some selfish motive in your own heart. What is idolatry? It's when you put something above God in your life. It's when you are more devoted to something than God. That could be a job, a relationship, money, etc. So these prophets of Baal will use divination to tap into the idolatry in your own heart and prophesy words that confirm what you really want to hear.

On the other hand, prophets of Jezebel are influenced by the spirit of Ashtoreth. Ashtoreth was the pagan god Queen Jezebel served. Ashtoreth was known as a seducing goddess of war. The prophets of Jezebel prophesy smooth, flattering words to try to manipulate and control you. If that doesn't work, they transition into warfare mode and prophesy fearful sayings to try to intimidate and control you. Ashtoreth and Baal were married. So these spirits often share one another's characteristics. We must discern what we are dealing with.

Baal prophets and Jezebel prophets are false prophets. What is a false prophet? In New Testament times a false prophet is not a prophet who prophesies a word that doesn't hit the target. A false prophet is one who sets out to deceive or who is so deceived themselves they prophesy falsely. You've heard that saying, "Oh, what a tangled web we weave when first we practice to deceive." I liken that tangled web to the workings of witchcraft. False prophets many times are tapping into divination, which is essentially witchcraft.

Then, of course, there are the prophets of Jehovah—the true prophets of the one true living God. I don't believe most false prophets start off as false prophets. I believe most false prophets fall into deception through the lust of the eyes, the lust of the flesh, or the pride of life (see 1 John 2:16).

# Characteristics of False Prophets

As we explore the characteristics of false prophets, keep in mind every false prophet is not necessarily going to manifest all of these traits—and manifesting one or even a few of these traits does not automatically make a false prophet. Every human being has character issues God is working on, and He perfects us as we grow in grace. Don't use this information to go on a witch hunt based on suspicion. Suspicion blocks discernment.

What we're about to discuss are collective traits—and I am sure there are more. You are going to notice a lot of these characteristics of false prophets are parallel to works of the flesh. This is why prophets—and all believers for that matter—need to crucify the flesh, especially as mouthpieces for God. Let's review the works of the flesh versus the fruit of the Spirit in Galatians 5:16-25.

> *I say then, walk in the Spirit, and you shall not fulfill the lust of the flesh. For the flesh lusts against the Spirit, and the Spirit against the flesh. These are in opposition to one another, so that you may not do the things that you please. But if you are led by the Spirit, you are not under the law.*
>
> *Now the works of the flesh are revealed, which are these: adultery, sexual immorality, impurity, lewdness, idolatry, sorcery, hatred, strife, jealousy, rage, selfishness, dissensions, heresies, envy, murders, drunkenness, carousing, and the like. I warn you, as I previously warned you, that those who do such things shall not inherit the kingdom of God.*

*But the fruit of the Spirit is love, joy, peace, patience, gentleness, goodness, faith, meekness, and self-control; against such there is no law. Those who are Christ's have crucified the flesh with its passions and lusts. If we live in the Spirit, let us also walk in the Spirit* (MEV).

Remember, Jesus said, "Beware of false prophets, who come to you in sheep's clothing, but inwardly they are ravenous wolves. You will know them by their fruits" (Matt. 7:15-16). The following 18 points are fruit of false prophets.

### *Daring Deceitfulness*

Deceit is the currency of false prophethood. Remember, a false prophet sets out to deceive. I believe they are among those Paul calls out to Timothy: "But evil men and seducers will grow worse and worse, deceiving and being deceived" (2 Tim. 3:13 MEV). I believe their conscience is seared like a hot iron as they speak lies in hypocrisy (see 1 Tim. 4:2). False prophets are among the "deceitful workers" of whom Paul warned the church at Corinth (see 2 Cor. 11:13).

Jesus said, "And many false prophets will rise and will deceive many" (Matt. 24:11 MEV). *Deceive* means "to be false to; to fail to fulfill; to cheat; to cause to accept as true or valid what is false or invalid." That's the undercurrent of a false prophet. Everything a false prophet does flows out of the river of deception rather than the river of truth—from the father of lies rather than the Spirit of truth.

False prophets are expert deceivers. Deception, essentially, is causing someone to believe something that is not true. False prophets are duplicitous, working in prophetic disinformation with cunning dupery. Many have experimented with what pulls on heart strings and positions someone to fall headlong into their prophetic trickery. Like the devil himself, they observe human behavior and look for weak spots—then strike with prophetic double-dealing.

## Savvy Seduction

False prophets deal in seduction. This is not relegated to the realm of sexual favors. Seduction goes beyond sex. Jesus said, "For false Christs and false prophets shall rise, and shall shew signs and wonders, to seduce, if it were possible, even the elect" (Mark 13:22 KJV). The word *seduce* in that verse comes from the Greek word *apoplanao*, which means "to cause to go astray, to lead away from the truth to error, to go astray, to stay away from."

Seduction is part of the deception. Jezebel's prophets, in particular, operate in this flow. They flatter you so they can beguile you. They entice you so they can delude you. They bait you so they can hook you. They coax you so they can trap you. You have to ask yourself this question: What is my price? If you have a price, Jezebel's prophets will find it and use it to seduce you.

Jesus said, "For false christs and false prophets will rise and show great signs and wonders to deceive, if possible, even the elect" (Matt. 24:24). No one is above falling into this trap, but we can protect ourselves by staying rooted and grounded in the Word of God. We must purge ourselves of the lust of the eyes, the lust of the flesh, and the pride of life (see 1 John 2:16).

## Merchandising the Saints

The love of money is a root of all evil (see 1 Tim. 6:10). False prophets are usually associated with merchandising the saints—also known as fleecing the sheep, also known as prophetic pickpocketing. Put another way, false prophets are all about the money, money, money, money. Yes, it takes money to do ministry, but people who pursue ministry for money are ill-motivated and open themselves up to the temptation to bow to the so-called "almighty dollar" instead of the Almighty God.

False prophets aggressively market false miracles, offer manipulative prophetic words, and fabricate testimonies to steal your hard-earned money out of your pocket. These wily workmen operate in hype rather than anointing. We see false prophets merchandising people in the Old and New Testaments:

> Her leaders judge for a bribe, her priests teach for a price, and her prophets practice divination for money (Micah 3:11 MEV).

> But there were also false prophets among the people, just as there will be false teachers among you, who will secretly bring in destructive heresies, even denying the Lord who bought them, bringing swift destruction upon themselves. And many will follow their destructive ways, because of whom the way of truth will be blasphemed. And in their greed they will exploit you with deceptive words (2 Peter 2:1-3 MEV).

When anyone is focused more on money than on Jesus, it should be a red flag to you. Yes, ministries have to take up offerings. But when people start calling out specific amounts in exchange for specific breakthroughs and blessings, know that something is wrong. You can sow a faith seed, but you can't buy a blessing. Jesus paid the price so you don't have to.

## Coveting Carnivores

The Lord spoke those somber words through Jeremiah, who goes down in Bible history as the weeping prophet: "For from the least of them even to the greatest of them, everyone is given to covetousness And from the prophet even to the priest, everyone deals falsely" (Jer. 6:13 MEV). What an indictment!

The Hebrew word for *covetousness* in that verse is *betsa*. It means "profit, unjust gain, gain (profit) acquired by violence." False prophets are violent in their pursuit of what you have. They crave what they don't have, but they don't trust God or wait for Him to supply it. Covetousness often has to do with money, but not always. Some false prophets covet your position, your anointing, and your spouse. Simon the Sorceror coveted what the true apostles had:

> *When Simon saw that through the laying on of the apostles' hands the Holy Spirit was given, he offered them money, saying, "Give me this power also, that anyone on whom I lay hands may receive the Holy Spirit"* (Acts 8:18-19).

The Bible speaks against covetousness over and over again. The only positive connotation for coveting in the Bible is with regard to prophecy. We are to covet to prophesy (see 1 Cor. 14:39). Burning to hear and share the true word of the Lord is different from burning to share a false prophecy for greedy gain.

## Corrupted Character

Paul, inspired by the Spirit of God, made it plain: "Do not be deceived: 'Bad company corrupts good morals'" (1 Cor. 15:33 MEV). It's clear that you can be deceived by a false prophet by spending too much time around them. I believe the Holy Spirit gives us checks in our spirit, but if we ignore the discernment He's manifesting in our heart we grow numb to that conviction and can wind up deceived and even defending the false prophet others are trying to warn us about.

It's vital for Christians to surround themselves with people of good character—and especially those speaking for God. Paul speaks of those who "corrupt the word of God" (2 Cor. 2:17 KJV). Other versions say "peddle" the Word of God. False prophets profane the prophetic word of God for profits. Character matters. I'm not talking about character flaws that are being worked out with fear and trembling. I'm speaking of corrupted character. *Merriam-Webster* defines *corruption* as "dishonest or illegal behavior especially by powerful people" and "a departure from the original or from what is pure or correct."[1]

### Spew False Prophetic Words

False prophets prophesy without an unction from the Lord. Put differently, false prophets know they have not heard from the Lord but prophesy anyway—or they are just totally deceived and actually believe the familiar spirit they are hearing is God. They prophesy what the people want to hear rather than what the Spirit of God is saying. Usually, they know God didn't say it, but they are saying it anyway. The Lord says:

> *See, I am against those who prophesy false dreams, says the Lord, and recount them and cause My people to err by their lies and reckless boasting. Yet I sent them not nor commanded them. Therefore they shall not profit this people at all, says the Lord* (Jeremiah 23:32 MEV).

### Unfaithful Covenant-Breakers

False prophets can't keep covenant. They may talk covenant but they can't walk covenant—except, perhaps, with other false prophets. You will notice false prophets move from camp to camp or alignment to alignment and not know why. Beware when you see prophets network-hopping or those who have had four spiritual fathers in three years. Something is wrong. God is a God of covenant.

The Lord spoke these sad words through Jeremiah:

> *I have seen also among the prophets of Jerusalem a horrible thing. They commit adultery and walk in lies. They also strengthen the hands of evildoers, so that no one repents from his wickedness. All of them are as Sodom to Me and her inhabitants as Gomorrah* (Jeremiah 23:14 MEV).

False prophets are not faithful to the Lord—or anyone else. They are out for their own good. They will consistently break their word and walk in circles with other evildoers. Companies of false prophets are rising, and they will defend each other with a vengeance.

### Serving the Father of Lies

False prophets are acting like their father—the father of lies. The devil offers false prophecy to us all the time—he whispers lies to us and releases vain imaginations. False prophets lie even when there is no reason to lie.

Ezekiel scribed these astonishing words: "Her prophets have daubed them with whitewash, seeing vanity and divining lies for them, saying, 'Thus says the Lord God,' when the Lord has not spoken" (Ezek. 22:28 MEV). Notice how these false prophets aren't just telling lies, they are actually divining lies. That's a whole different level of lies. These false prophets were practicing witchcraft and many believed them.

I think we all know what a lie is, but let's look at a definition from Dictionary.com anyway to drive the point home: "a false statement made with deliberate intent to deceive; an intentional untruth; a falsehood; something intended or serving to convey a false impression; imposture; to speak falsely or utter untruth knowingly, as with intent to deceive."[2]

How can you discern someone is "prophe-lying" (lying about a prophetic word they receive)? The more you know the truth—the more of a student of the Word you are—the easier it is to discern prophetic witchcraft. Be a lover of the truth.

### Drunkeness and Loose Living

False prophets may live a loose life. Some call it "sloppy agape." They are loose with eating, loose with drinking, loose with sexual encounters. I don't believe you should see a prophet in the club getting drunk on Saturday night then prophesying over nations the next morning in church. It's a character issue.

Isaiah prophesied these words of the Lord:

> But they also have erred through wine and stagger from strong drink; the priest and the prophet have erred through strong drink, they are confused by wine, they stagger from strong drink; they err while having visions, they stumble when rendering judgment (Isaiah 28:7 MEV).

Prophets who live loose open themselves up to error. Would you want an inebriated prophet prophesying over your destiny? How about a prophet with a hangover? Do you want a seer releasing visual revelation he received while bowing to Budweiser? You may not see prophets erring through strong drink because you don't see their lifestyles, but then again you might. I have smelled alcohol on them. My nose did the discerning for me.

## Foolishness and Quarrelsome

False prophets act a fool and are argumentative. They like to debate over what is clear Bible truth, often to avoid accountability or defend their deviant practices.

> *The days of visitation are come, the days of recompence are come; Israel shall know it: the prophet is a fool, the spiritual man is mad, for the multitude of thine iniquity, and the great hatred* (Hosea 9:7 KJV).

The Hebrew word for *fool* in that verse is *eviyl*. It means "be foolish, of one who despises wisdom, of one who mocks when guilty, of one who is quarrelsome, of one who is licentious." The Bible has plenty to say about the foolish man. False prophets have rejected the Lord's wisdom, will not receive correction when caught, and will breed strife and engage in immorality.

## Propagate Heresies

Some false prophets propagate heresies. There's the "no spiritual warfare heresy" that demands we don't have to battle principalities and powers as Paul clearly described in Ephesians 6. Then there's the hyper-grace heresy that insists repentance is a once-and-for all issue and we can live how we want because we are not under the law but under grace. These are two of many heresies false prophets, over the ages, have forwarded.

Dictionary.com defines *heresy* as "opinion or doctrine at variance with the orthodox or accepted doctrine, especially of a church or religious system."[3] Heresies defy the Word of God. False prophets propagate heresies that can lead you away from the truth that sets you free. Most often, this heresy benefits them personally by excusing a character flaw or causing people to pledge undying allegiance to their cult (ministry). This is nothing new. Peter warned:

> *But there were also false prophets among the people, just as there will be false teachers among you, who will secretly bring in destructive heresies, even denying the Lord who bought them, bringing swift destruction upon themselves* (2 Peter 2:1 MEV).

The word *heresies* comes from the Greek word *hairesis*, which means, in this context, "dissensions arising from diversity of opinions and aims." The King James Version says "damnable heresies." The Greek word for *damnable* in that verse means "destroying, utter destruction, the destruction which consists of eternal misery in hell," according to the *KJV New Testament Greek Lexicon*.

### Move in Deadly Presumptions

False prophets often move in presumption. *Presume* means to form an opinion from little or no evidence and to take something as true or as fact without actual proof. False prophets prophesy out of what they presume are the desires of your heart based on who you came to the meeting with (or without), how you dress, or even your age and ethnicity. Another way to say it is false prophets stereotype people and prophesy to the stereotype.

False prophets may presume people who come to a meeting alone want to be married, for example, and prophesy mates. I've seen false prophets do this when their husband was actually in the bathroom. False prophets may presume women want more children. I stood and watched a false prophet prophesy to a woman nearly 50 that God was going to give her more children. That's not impossible, but also not likely. False prophets make soulish presumptions of this nature and crush hope.

I noticed something extremely interesting while studying about presumption. The definition of *presume* and the definition of *prejudice* are extremely similar, and closer reflection offers up some important insights into the poison of presumption. Some definitions of the word *prejudice* include a "preconceived judgment or opinion or an adverse opinion or leaning formed without just grounds or before sufficient knowledge."

While the King James Version of the Bible only mentions the words *presume, presumed, presumptuous,* and *presumptuously* eleven times, the act almost always leads to the death. Indeed, there are few things worse than a presumptuous prophet. Deuteronomy 18:20 declares, "The prophet who presumes to speak a word in My name, which I have not commanded him to speak, or who speaks in the name of other gods, that prophet shall die." Again, we're living in an age of grace, but God still hates presumption.

### *Irresponsible in Prophetic Ministry*

False prophets are irresponsible. They don't care what kind of mess they leave in the host pastor's church or the devastation their false directional prophetic utterances bring to the lives of those they are prophesying to. False prophets release irresponsible words without fear of repercussion, then move on to the next victims after collecting offerings from unsuspecting sheep desperate for a word from the Lord.

In Zephaniah 3:4, "The prophets are irresponsible and treacherous; the priests defile what is sacred, and twist the law of God to their own advantage" (GNT). The New Living Translation puts it this way: "Its prophets are arrogant liars seeking their own gain." And *The Message* says, "Her prophets are out for what they can get. They're opportunists—you can't trust them."

### *Murdering Reputations*

Most prophets aren't cold-blooded killers in today's world. But they will kill your dreams by having you chase idols. And they murder reputations of others, especially true prophets who discern them. Jezebelic false prophets are masters of this tactic.

Consider these sobering words from Jeremiah:

> *Yet it happened because of the sins of her prophets and the sins of her priests, who defiled the city by shedding innocent blood. They wandered blindly through the streets, so defiled by blood that no one dared touch them* (Lamentations 4:13-14 NLT).

### *Cursing and Judgment*

False prophets spew curses and judgments. God is a God of judgment, but any prophet who is truly speaking for the Lord would be broken over this, like Jeremiah, the weeping prophet. False prophets take pleasure in releasing words of judgment, especially against individuals who have defied them. False prophets will say things like, "This man will die in thirty days because he did not receive my truth."

This is essentially a curse and it's dangerous not only to the false prophet and target of the curse but also to those who come into agreement with it. False prophets issue harsh curses on Facebook and people cheer them on, not realizing that they are sowing cursing, grieving the Holy Spirit, and find that curses can land on them if they don't repent.

> *Out of the same mouth proceed blessing and cursing. My brothers, these things ought not to be so. Does a spring yield at the same opening sweet and bitter water? Can the fig tree, my brothers, bear olives, or a vine, figs? So no spring can yield both salt water and fresh water* (James 3:10-12 MEV).

New Testament prophets edify, comfort, and exhort—not curse. King Balak hired the false prophet to curse the people of God and he could not (see Num. 22:6-7). Romans 12:14 tells us plainly to bless and curse not.

### Treacherous Traitors

Zephaniah 3:4 says, "Her prophets are reckless, treacherous men; her priests have profaned the sanctuary and done violence to the law" (MEV). *Treacherous* in this verse means just what it says—treacherous. False prophets are false-hearted, proverbial snakes in the grass, unsound and unsafe.

False prophets are treacherous. *Merriam-Webster*'s dictionary defines *treacherous* as "likely to betray trust, unreliable, providing insecure footing or support, marked by hidden dangers, hazards or perils."[4] That about sums it up.

False prophets raise money for projects they never follow through with. They don't count the cost because they are not paying the price. They will betray their best friend to advance their ministry. They make grand promises for the future they don't intend to keep in order to get what they want in the here and now.

### Stealing Prophetic Words

I've witnessed for many years a troubling trend in the prophetic movement—a trend that is proliferating among pontificating voices who parrot true prophets. Essentially, there's a lot of plagiarism in the prophetic.

"See, therefore I am against the prophets, says the Lord, who steal My words, each from his neighbor. See, I am against the prophets, says the Lord, who use their tongues and say, 'The Lord says'" (Jer. 23:30-31 MEV). Not only will false prophets steal money out of your pocket, they steal prophecies from true and false prophets alike. I've seen this on the Internet time and time again.

It's been said imitation is the highest form of flattery. But to imitate someone's prophetic word as if you got it straight out of a "profound prophetic dream," a throne room experience, or a still small voice coming unto you isn't flattery. It's a falsehood.

While I know all too well that God speaks to many different prophetic voices about the exact same word, Scripture, or theme, I am convinced prophetic plagiarists are acting like high-schoolers who didn't have time to read their literature assignment and are depending on CliffsNotes instead.

### Operate in False Anointing

Remember, Jesus said, "For false christs and false prophets will arise and show great signs and wonders to deceive, if possible, even the elect" (Matt. 24:24 MEV). These false ministers must be pretty convincing if they can deceive God's very elect— or the elect must be lacking in discernment. Signs and wonders to not validate a ministry. Magicians in the Old Testament offered signs and wonders.

## Many Manifestations of False Prophets

I can't possibly list all the earmarks of a false prophet. I probably haven't experienced them all. But here are a few more behaviors to watch for. I would caution you to use discernment and not make presumptions yourself because you don't like someone's preaching, clothing style, or culture.

Jezebel is an information seeker. Jezebelic false prophets scout social media, looking for personal information so they can "prophesy" to the soul of an unsuspecting person, hoping to build a soul tie. They inquire about personal information in one-on-one conversations and pry for information about others so they can prey on them.

False prophets twist the Word of God, especially Scriptures on giving, for their own greedy gain with no thought of how the sower will struggle after donating into rotten soil. False prophets avoid accountability and any form of correction. False prophets are braggadocious, making sure everyone knows when they are accurate but failing to blow that same trumpet when they clearly missed the mark.

False prophets usually run in companies of false prophets, sharing conference space and supporting one another. They surround themselves with yes-men and weak-minded people who do not know the Word of God and don't believe they can accurately hear the voice of God for themselves. False prophets validate themselves, often insist on titles, and they rarely, if ever, call for repentance.

I've seen false prophets rising, and Christian crowds cheering them on. A prophet once invited me to speak at a meeting in Texas. I didn't know him, so I asked a few other people I did know if they could vouch for him. One person I trusted assured me he was on major Christian television networks and that he was on the up and up. When I went to his meeting, something was clearly off. I tried to give him the benefit of the doubt, but as the meetings went on everything was about money, money, money.

This prophet was known for money miracles. I believe in money miracles, but if money is the only thing you talk about then you've left Jesus out of the equation. The full gospel is about more than money. This false prophet pressured, pushed, and cajoled everyone to sow a large seed, promising immediate money miracles and weight-loss miracles the following night. He was forceful about it, even telling the ushers to lock the doors so no one could leave.

After people sowed, he told them to check their purse, check their wallet and check their bank account. As I looked around the sanctuary, I could see the disappointment when these deceived donors found there was no miracle or increase, except for the false prophet who duped them. One woman started screaming. I thought to myself, "She has figured out this is a scam." No, she actually thought she had received a money miracle. In tears, the woman testified how she had sowed her last four dollars into the offering and immediately found a wadded up one dollar bill with Cheetos on it in her purse. (I'm not even kidding.) She was crying hysterically over this "miracle."

Now, I'm not the best at math, but I do know this. Sowing four dollars and getting one dollar back is not a miracle. It's not a harvest on a seed. It's not the multiplication effect the false prophet promised. The crowd cheered the false prophet on. My jaw dropped. My spirit was grieved. I left the meeting disgusted. The false prophet later sent me a paltry offering via PayPal. He emailed and said the meeting didn't bear the financial fruit he had hoped. I replied, "I guess you didn't get your money miracle."

## NOTES

1. Merriam-Webster, s.v. "Corruption," https://www.merriam
   -webster.com/dictionary/corruption.
2. Dictionary.com, s.v. "Lie," https://www.dictionary.com/browse/
   lie?s=t.
3. Dictionary.com, s.v. "Heresy," https://www.dictionary.com/
   browse/heresy?s=t.
4. Merriam-Webster, s.v. "Treacherous," https://www.merriam
   -webster.com/dictionary/treacherous.

# CHAPTER 4

# FALSE PROPHETS VS. FALSE PROPHECY

C an false prophets release true prophecy? Can true prophets release false prophecy? These are important distinctions in prophetic dimensions. Many are confused because they judge the prophet based on the message alone rather than the spirit behind the words.

When someone prophesies to me, I am not listening as closely to the words coming out of their mouth. I can record the word and review it later. When someone prophesies to me, rather, I am discerning the spirit behind the words. That's because, yes, a false prophet can release a true prophecy and, yes, a true prophet can release a false prophecy (in the sense that if the prophecy is not true, it's false). But I don't want a word from an accurate diviner.

Here's a key to understanding what is happening behind the scenes of these prophetic operations: When false prophets release a true prophecy, the source wasn't God but a spirit of divination. When a true prophet releases a false prophecy (or as some put it, a poor prophecy), they are not typically tapping into divination. We'll talk more about how true prophets miss it later in this chapter.

## Prophecy Is Fallible

The Word of God never fails and is inerrant (see Matt. 24:35). Prophecy is fallible because prophets are fallible. Anyone can miss it. In the Old Testament, if a prophet uttered a prophecy that didn't turn out to be true, he was deemed a false prophet. Thankfully, that is not so in the New Testament. Thank God we don't have to worry about getting stoned if we miss it!

Again, prophecy is fallible. Even the most mature Christians who are rooted and grounded in the love of Christ and the Word of God can and do offer prophetic utterances that are less than 100 percent accurate. As believers, we must learn to judge prophetic words, which we'll dive into more in a later chapter. The Bible makes a case for the reality that prophecy can be flawed or downright false.

Paul wrote: "Let two or three prophets speak, and let the others judge" (1 Cor. 14:29). And again, "He who is spiritual judges all things" (1 Cor. 2:15). John wrote: "Beloved, do not believe every spirit, but test the spirits, whether they are of God; because many false prophets have gone out into the world" (1 John 4:1).

If it were impossible for one who is truly gifted by the Holy Spirit to release an inaccurate prophecy, Paul and John would not have exhorted us to judge prophetic words. There would be no need to judge the prophecy. We could just accept it as truth. We must be careful, then, not only to judge what we receive or hear in public settings through the mouths of others, but also to be responsible enough to judge what we hear in our own hearts. The Bible says the heart is deceitful above all things and desperately wicked (see Jer. 17:9).

Consider this: Wayne Grudem, a theologian and author, says prophecy in ordinary New Testament churches was not equal to Scripture in authority, but was simply a very human and sometimes partially mistaken report of something the Holy Spirit brought to someone's mind.

Mike Bickle, director of the International House of Prayer-Kansas City, explains that, "The Spirit conveys to our mind thoughts we communicate in contemporary language. They are a mixture of God's words and man's words that combine divine inspiration and with the human process. Some prophetic words may be 10 percent God's words and 90 percent man's word while others have a greater revelatory content. Most prophecy has a strong mixture of man's ideas."

While many words are extremely accurate, then, we must make room for the possibility that someone's own thoughts, experiences, biases, and emotions can influence their prophetic utterances. With that admission, we must carefully weed through prophetic words—especially those that could impact people profoundly for better or worse—for traces of our human influence.

## The Agabus Prophecy

Prophecy is filtered through the human soul, with all its emotions, reasoning, and intellect. You might say there is an art and a science to prophecy. Intimacy with God and prayer is the art while

speaking forth the ideas God reveals to our hearts is a science—
and it's an imperfect science because we are imperfect people.

What New Testament Scripture proves the point that prophecy can originate from the Holy Spirit but be clouded by man's
filter? The Agabus prophecy in Acts 21. Paul was on his way to
Jerusalem when a prophet named Agabus—mind you, the Bible
calls him a prophet—offered Paul a warning. Let's listen in:

> *And as we stayed many days, a certain prophet named
> Agabus came down from Judea. When he had come to
> us, he took Paul's belt, bound his own hands and feet,
> and said, "Thus says the Holy Spirit, 'So shall the Jews at
> Jerusalem bind the man who owns this belt, and deliver
> him into the hands of the Gentiles'"* (Acts 21:10-11).

That was the prophecy. But what actually happened? When
we look at the account in Scripture, we find it turned out a little
differently than Agabus prophesied. Paul was indeed arrested in
Jerusalem, but not by the Jews. Let's read on:

> *Then Paul took the men, and the next day, having been
> purified with them, entered the temple to announce the
> expiration of the days of purification, at which time an
> offering should be made for each one of them.*
>
> *Now when the seven days were almost ended, the Jews
> from Asia, seeing him in the temple, stirred up the whole
> crowd and laid hands on him, crying out, "Men of Israel,
> help! This is the man who teaches all men everywhere
> against the people, the law, and this place; and further-
> more he also brought Greeks into the temple and has*

*defiled this holy place." (For they had previously seen Trophimus the Ephesian with him in the city, whom they supposed that Paul had brought into the temple.)*

*And all the city was disturbed; and the people ran together, seized Paul, and dragged him out of the temple; and immediately the doors were shut. Now as they were seeking to kill him, news came to the commander of the garrison that all Jerusalem was in an uproar. He immediately took soldiers and centurions, and ran down to them. And when they saw the commander and the soldiers, they stopped beating Paul. Then the commander came near and took him, and commanded him to be bound with two chains; and he asked who he was and what he had done. And some among the multitude cried one thing and some another* (Acts 21:26-34).

Now, let's explore how Agabus' original prophecy compared to what actually happened to Paul in Jerusalem: Whom did Agabus prophesy would bind Paul in Jerusalem? Who arrested Paul in Jerusalem? What part did the Jews play in Paul's arrest? What do we typically call what Agabus did when he bound his own hands and feet as he released the prophetic word?

As you can see in considering the answers to those questions, Agabus' prophecy was not 100 percent accurate. Agabus said the Holy Spirit told him that the Jews and Jerusalem would bind the man who owned the belt that he bound himself with. But that's not what happened. So it's clear that the Holy Spirit didn't speak these exact words to Agabus. The Holy Spirit is never wrong, so if the Holy Spirit actually told Agabus that the Jews would bind Paul, then it would have happened that way.

That said, the general word that Agabus gave was accurate. The bottom line was that Paul was arrested in Jerusalem, just by the Romans instead of by the Jews. And the Jews played a key role in that arrest by creating such stir at seeing Paul in the temple. The Roman soldiers had to respond—and so they did.

Now, Agabus was known as an accurate prophet. This Agabus is the same Agabus we find in Acts 11:28 prophesying a famine in the land, which also happened in the days of Claudius Caesar. Agabus was not a false prophet, but as a New Testament prophet he is not functioning in the same role as an Old Testament prophet— and neither are we as prophets or prophetic people.

## Nathan Flat-Out Missed It

Indeed, even in Old Testament times, we see God's grace in prophetic ministry. I'm reminded of the time David was dwelling in his house meditating upon the Lord. God had given him rest from all his enemies. David was talking with the prophet Nathan—the same prophet who later would rebuke him for committing adultery with Bathsheba and setting up the murder of her husband, Uriah the Hittite (see 2 Sam. 12). David was dismayed because God was dwelling inside tent curtains while he lived in a house of cedar (see 2 Sam. 7:2).

That's when Nathan spoke these words from his anointed mouth: "Go, do all that is in your heart, for the Lord is with you" (2 Sam. 7:3). Although this wasn't a "thus saith the Lord" type of prophetic word, it was a word of approval from a trusted prophetic voice in David's life. David was looking for prophetic counsel about his plans to build a house for the Lord, seeking confirmation that it was in God's will. David seemed to receive that confirmation, but the Lord took steps to correct Nathan's pure-hearted mistake before the king got too far.

God sent Nathan back to David with a bona fide prophetic word that contradicted his friendly counsel to "do all that is in your heart, for the Lord is with you." The Lord did not want David to build him a house but rather committed to establishing David's throne forever (see 2 Sam. 7:4-17). What did Nathan do? He went back to David and corrected himself. Imagine if he didn't?

There are two lessons we can learn from this incident. First, if you flow in prophetic ministry, you have to be careful not to accidentally lead people astray by sharing your opinion without a disclaimer— and sometimes even with a disclaimer. If you are a believer who hangs around with prophets, be careful to discern if they are speaking for the Lord or from their own opinion. Ask them if you aren't sure.

How did Nathan miss it? Did he even hear from the Lord to begin with? Was he offering his wisdom instead of the wisdom of the Lord? Was he trying to appease David in his heart's desire? Did he do it for political or friendship reasons? We don't know. It could have been one of these reasons or more than one of these reasons. All of these are pitfalls in prophetic ministry.

## Does the Holy Spirit Always Speak Expressly or Not?

For all the dramatic prophetic encounters you hear or read about— such as the audible voice of the Lord or angels appearing—most prophecy comes to believers in a subtler way, though a still small voice, symbolic dreams, or faint impressions. The Holy Spirit speaks to us in many ways, but in our day-to-day lives it's typically a knowing or a few words spoken to our heart.

Some have taught that the "Holy Spirit speaks expressly" in relation to prophetic ministry, based on First Timothy 4:1-3. Although the Holy Spirit is certainly capable of making Himself clear, these verses are specifically referring to a passage Paul, inspired by the Holy Spirit, wrote in the New Testament about the end times. The entire passage reads:

> *Now the Spirit expressly says that in latter times some will depart from the faith, giving heed to deceiving spirits and doctrines of demons, speaking lies in hypocrisy, having their own conscience seared with a hot iron, forbidding to marry, and commanding to abstain from foods which God created to be received with thanksgiving by those who believe and know the truth* (1 Timothy 4:1-3).

Paul was saying here that the Holy Spirit spoke this to him expressly about a great apostasy. The Holy Spirit told him clearly (NLT). He distinctly and expressly declared it (AMPC). Paul was penning Scripture, and the Holy Spirit spoke expressly. Keep in mind that prophecy is not on the same level as Scripture. No new Scripture is being written. Prophetic words must be submitted to the written Word of God.

All that said, God is able to make Himself clear. Prophetic words should not be so ambiguous that they could mean anything to anyone. If a prophet is prophesying, the word should not be so generic that it would be hard to tell if it ever came to pass.

Prophets who prophesy ambiguous generic words—or words so vague you can't tell how to apply them—are often not hearing from the Holy Spirit but are divining seducing words.

# Seven Ways Prophets Miss it

I don't believe anyone is 100 percent accurate 100 percent of the time because although God communicates clearly, we interpret and share it in our language through our human perspectives and even biases. So how do we miss it? Here are a few other thoughts:

### 1. *Prophets can miss it because people take their words as the Word of God.*

If people know someone is a prophet, they may seek advice and take the prophet's words as prophetic in nature even if the prophet is just sharing their opinion from experience or natural wisdom. In this way, a prophet could accidentally lead someone astray because the inquirer is so desperate for a word from God that they take anything the prophet says as a prophecy.

This is not the prophet's fault, though I believe prophets should be clear as to when it is their counsel and when it is the counsel of the Lord. For example, when Paul gave advice to widows on remarrying, he said: "But in my opinion it would be better for her to stay single, and I think I am giving you counsel from God's Spirit when I say this" (1 Cor. 7:40 NLT). Seasoned prophets will tell you if they are speaking their own mind or the mind of Christ. While it's not wrong to go to prophets for counsel, believers must develop a relationship with Jesus and seek His counsel first.

## 2. Prophets can miss it because prophets are imperfect.

The only perfect prophet was Jesus. We are not sinless like He was, and therefore we are prone to pressures, prejudices, and party lines. The authority of the prophetic words prophets release does not depend on the prophet's own perfection, but the prophet's character can certainly hinder our prophetic ministry. When prophets insist they never miss it, they have already missed it. Pride comes before a prophetic fall.

## 3. Human language is imperfect.

Sometimes prophets get impressions about things but human language is not sufficient to describe what the prophet saw or is sensing or feeling. When the prophet jumps out too quickly to try to verbalize an impression, it can lead to error. When a seasoned prophet tries to describe what they are sensing—and at times they must—they couch it with the caveat that they may not be using the right words. Mature prophets pray impressions through before discussing them publicly and continue praying until they understand more fully what the Lord is trying to say. That is not always possible, but is ideal.

## 4. The prophet's theology is imperfect.

I believe when we get to heaven, there will be points of theology in all of our lives that we discover are wrong. Many of us have been taught wrong things—and we don't know what we don't know. Wrong theology can infiltrate prophecies if we are not cautious. By the same token, a prophetic word can be accurate and rock our theology.

## 5. *The prophet's revelation of Jesus is imperfect.*

The revelation the prophet has of Jesus Himself tempers the release of prophecy. If the prophet sees Jesus as a loving, graceful God who is full of mercy, our prophecies will come from that flow. If the prophet sees Jesus as an angry God who is judging us, our prophecies will often carry that tone.

## 6. *The prophet's dream interpretation is imperfect.*

Dreams and visions can be difficult to interpret or apply accurately. In sharing a dream, the prophet may leave out important details of what they saw in a dream or vision or, again, interpret that dream or vision through a lens clouded by their own perspectives.

## 7. *The prophet's faith is imperfect.*

The Bible says we prophesy according to the proportion of our faith (see Rom. 12:6). No one's faith has been perfected. If the prophet moves beyond his faith in his prophetic utterances, he can tap into the idolatry in someone's heart, our own soul, or witchcraft.

Paul exhorted believers who flowed in the gift of prophecy to use that gift in proportion to their faith. But what does that mean? According to the Reformation Study Bible:

> Some interpreters see "faith" as the prophet's own faith. Others understand "faith" to mean the truth content of the gospel as the standard and measure of each prophetic utterance, testing whether the utterance conforms to the "pattern of sound words" (2 Tim. 1:13).[1]

# A Word on Judging Prophecy

I wrote an entire book on this—*Did the Spirit of God Say That? 27 Ways to Judge Prophecy.* If you want to learn more on this topic, it's a thorough read. I broke the book down into five categories: Bible-based tests, fruit-based tests, clarity-based tests, Spirit-based tests, and character-based tests.

I can't rehash all of those tests here, but you should be aware of some of the most critical means of judging prophecy. For example, is the prophecy in line with Scriptures? It's important to study to show yourself approved so you can rightly divide the word of truth. If you don't now the Word of God, you are less likely to recognize false prophecy. The Holy Ghost doesn't contradict Himself.

> *This is He who came by water and blood—Jesus Christ. He did not come by water only, but by water and blood. It is the Spirit who bears witness, because the Spirit is the truth. There are three who testify in heaven: the Father, the Word, and the Holy Spirit, and the three are one. There are three that testify on earth: the Spirit, the water, and the blood, and the three are toward the one* (1 John 5:6-8 MEV).

Do the prophecies produce liberty? Where the spirit of the Lord is, there is liberty (see 2 Cor. 3:17). Remember, "For you have not received the spirit of slavery again to fear. But you have received the Spirit of adoption, by whom we cry, 'Abba, Father'" (Rom. 8:15 MEV). Does the prophecy seek to control? God gave us a free will. He doesn't try to control us. Does the prophecy breed fear? God does not give us a spirit of fear (see 2 Tim. 1:7).

The prophecy may bring about a fear of the Lord, a soberness—but not a demonic fear. Consider picking up a copy of the book to go deeper in this.

## NOTE

1. R.C. Sproul and Keith A. Mathison, *Reformation Study Bible* (Phillipsburg, NJ: P & R Publishing, 2005), 1634, footnote p.

# CHAPTER 5

# THE RISE OF PROPHETIC CULTS AND DIVINING PROPHETS

While raising up prophets and prophetic people that are bringing forth pure prophetic utterances in the nations, I've also been beating the drum about the rise of Jezebel and Baal prophets since 2001, writing boldly and warning the Body of Christ about the coming deluge of false prophets. Although I'm encouraged by much of what I see in the prophetic, I'm alarmed at the rapid rise of false prophets. I know I shouldn't be, because Jesus Himself prophesied the reality: "For false christs and false prophets will rise and show great signs and wonders to deceive, if possible, even the elect. See, I have told you beforehand" (Matt. 24:24-25). In *The Passion Translation*, verse 25 reads: "I prophesy it will happen!" Jesus, our Prototype Prophet, never missed it. Not once. And we're seeing this Scripture start to manifest before our eyes.

In 2016 while I was serving as editor of *Charisma* magazine, I labored to bring a prophetic mantle to the periodical. I wanted to use the platform and influence God gave me to demonstrate what the true prophetic looked like, in all its diversity. In that role I had the opportunity to speak with and get to know many prophetic leaders.

After discussing some grievous issues in modern prophetic ministry with two particular leaders in the Body of Christ, I felt a strong burden to pray—to enter intercession for emerging prophets and the prophetic movement in general. Because I was on print deadlines for *Charisma*—and because missing the deadline came with heavy printer costs that I was charged with avoiding—I politely suggested to the Lord it would be more convenient to pray later.

The Holy Spirit acted like He didn't hear me. He would not release me from the intercessory prayer burden. Yielding to the Spirit of God, I got down on my knees to pray, planning to press in for about five minutes and pick up where I left off after the printer deadlines were met. Or so I thought.

That five-minute prayer lasted over an hour and morphed into travail that left me on the hardwood floors of my condo weeping, sweating, and groaning in the spirit. I was lying in a puddle of my own tears as the Lord showed me the state of some camps in the modern-day prophetic movement. He gave me a glimpse into how the enemy wanted to pollute the prophetic with various forms of idolatry and immorality, deceive them with extra-biblical extremes, and tempt them to eat from Jezebel's table and ignite strange fire.

When the Lord showed me the next five years (this was in 2016) were vital for the prophetic movement, I was overwhelmed. What could I possible do to change this? I am just one person and God is raising up multiplied thousands of prophetic voices in the years ahead. The burden was so great I called two other major prophetic leaders in the Body of Christ to share my encounter and my concerns. They agreed that there were serious issues and a serious reset was needed. I knew I couldn't fix it all, but they gave me good advice: Do your part.

After much counsel, deliberation, and prayer, I launched my School of the Prophets, which offers prophetic training to all believers, in September 2016. In November of that same year, I launched the Ignite Network for prophets and prophetic people. Again, I know I can't solve all the issues in prophetic ministry, nor am I called to. But I must be faithful to do my part. I believe if we're all faithful to do what God has called us to do, we can see a healthier, stronger prophetic voice in the nations. My prayer is this book is also part of the solution.

## The Rise of Prophetic Cults

Cults are nothing new. Cults didn't start when the prophetic movement was birthed in the 1980s. But prophetic cults are forming. I'm not talking about Jim Jones-type cults that woo people into compounds where they ultimately commit suicide by drinking a flavored drink mixed with Valium, chloral hydrate, cyanide, and Phenergan. But prophetic cults are forming, mixing poisonous spiritual Kool-Aid and thirsty masses are drinking it voluntarily. That's in part because they haven't been equipped to hear from God themselves or they don't read their Bibles.

I have not dubbed myself the sheriff of the prophetic police force. I am not looking for something to criticize. I'm just passionate about the prophetic movement's maturity and purification.

It's been said the prophetic doesn't make people weird. That's not really true. The prophetic just reveals the weird that's already in them.

There's a particular group of false prophets whose name I won't mention because the devil loves lawsuits. These false prophets are all about money and fame. I shared one of their posts and warned people about them after I saw those who I thought were discerning people sowing large seeds. Soon, I started receiving death threats against me and rape threats against my daughter. To this day, they continue to call our ministry phone with pornographic messages and especially foul language. Clearly, these cultish prophets are demon-inspired.

Thank God, He is raising up strong prophetic churches full of the Spirit of God and equipped believers who are wise and understand the will of the Lord (see Eph. 5). There are more on God's side than on the enemy's side. While prophetic cults are forming, so are true companies of prophets. We must discern the difference.

Jezebel and Baal prophets don't want believers to hear from God for themselves because they would lose control. Therefore, they band together, nodding in agreement with one another's bitterness-backed prophecies and make a name for themselves on social media with some help from the prince of the power of the air.

I believe the root of prophetic cults—and any other type of cult—is bitterness. And it seems the only thing that soothes their pain is power, money, and fame. What makes me think that, you ask? Scripture's chronicle of Simon the sorcerer.

*Simon had practiced magic in the city, posing as a famous man and dazzling all the Samaritans with his wizardry. He had them all, from little children to old men, eating out of his hand. They all thought he had supernatural powers, and called him "the Great Wizard." He had been around a long time and everyone was more or less in awe of him* (Acts 8:9-11 MSG).

Here we see that old Simon the sorcerer was an imposter. He reveled in the attention the townspeople showered upon him. The King James translation of verse 10 reveals how the people respected him: "This man is the great power of God." So we see that Simon was a false prophet who had gained the trust of the people and probably called in financial favors in exchange for his magical powers. The fact that Simon had money in his pocket and thought it was convenient to buy and sell "power" is evidenced by a visit from the apostles Peter and John.

Philip's preaching apparently got Simon born again because the Bible says, "Simon himself also believed" and was baptized (Acts 8:13). After his conversion, he continued following Philip and observing the miracles and signs that were wrought at his hand. Then the apostles Peter and John showed up and brought the baptism of the Holy Ghost with them. They laid their hands on the people and these newly minted disciples freely received the Holy Spirit and the power that comes along with Him. Simon was awestruck by the demonstration of power at the hands of the apostles. He was amazed that the believers were speaking in other tongues and prophesying. That's about the time Simon made his dreadful mistake. He offered the apostles money in exchange for

Holy Ghost power (see Acts 8:18-19). He was met with a sharp rebuke from Peter.

> *When Simon saw that the apostles by merely laying on hands conferred the Spirit, he pulled out his money, excited, and said, "Sell me your secret! Show me how you did that! How much do you want? Name your price!" Peter said, "To hell with your money! And you along with it. Why, that's unthinkable—trying to buy God's gift! You'll never be part of what God is doing by striking bargains and offering bribes. Change your ways—and now! Ask the Master to forgive you for trying to use God to make money. I can see this is an old habit with you; you reek with money-lust"* (Acts 8:18-23 MSG).

The King James translation gets to the root of the matter, though. Peter says, "I perceive that thou art in the gall of bitterness, and in the bond of iniquity" (Acts 8:23). Gall is bile—that yellow-green viscid alkaline fluid the liver secrets and passes to the intestines. In other words, it goes to the gut. You could say Simon had a root of bitterness in his life. Bitterness is associated with unforgiveness after a severe hurt or wound that hasn't healed. Who knows what happened to Simon; who rejected him or hurt him? But being an occultist power-wielding big shot made him feel better about himself. When he got born again, he knew he had to put away his occultist powers but his ego still needed a lift, so he sought to buy the power of God and keep the people eating out of the palms of his hands.

The apostle James made it clear—a fountain can't put forth sweet and bitter water (see James 3:11). Rejection, hurts, and wounds—and the bitterness that may result in the wake of unforgiveness of the ones who caused them—can lead someone into prophetic divination. If misery loves company, then it's easy to see how companies of false prophets, a.k.a. prophetic cults, would wind up mingling together.

## Beware Bitter Prophets

Bitter prophets are rising, and some of it is the fault of a church who rejected them. Sometimes they are bitter because of abandonment issues in their childhood. They are influenced by an orphan spirit and feel prophecy is their road to acceptance. Some prophets have been betrayed. Regardless of the reason why we're seeing more bitterness polluting the prophetic, it's each individual's responsibility to keep their heart clean. The Holy Spirit is issuing a serious warning about bitter prophets. The Lord impressed these words on my heart:

> *"Beware the bitter prophets releasing bitter curses out of their bitter hearts. Pray for them, because their end will be bitter if they don't repent. They are bringing great harm to My Body with manipulative maneuvers that seduce, deceive, and derail. Don't come into agreement with the bitterness, lest you be defiled also. God shall not be mocked; whatever a man sows he will reap. Bless and do not curse."*

The Greek word for *bitter* in James 3:11 means "extreme wickedness; a bitter root, and so producing bitter fruit; and bitter hatred," according to *The KJV New Testament Greek Lexicon*. Bitterness is extremely wicked in the eyes of the Lord and correlates to hatred. It's no wonder that bitterness opens the door to demonic oppression. The bitter heart is a darkened heart. First John 2:11 says, "But whoever hates his brother is in darkness, and walks in darkness, and does not know where he is going, because the darkness has blinded his eyes" (MEV).

Bitterness, then, is connected to spiritual blindness and deception. That's why Paul warns the church at Ephesus to, "Let all bitterness, wrath, anger, outbursts, and blasphemies, with all malice, be taken away from you. And be kind one to another, tenderhearted, forgiving one another, just as God in Christ also forgave you" (Eph. 4:31-32 MEV). If you have bitterness in your heart, you won't discern a bitter divining prophet because you have common ground. Bitter prophets are gathering bitter people to themselves and leading them into greater deception.

I've talked to members of these prophetic cults. They pump each other's egos in every conversation. They spew forth prophecies that tap into the idolatry of people's hearts in prayer lines and prophesy judgments and curses out of the bitterness of their own—and they make money in the process. God loves these people and their self-deception surely grieves Him. What's important to remember is something in the hearts of these false prophetic ministers opened the door to the devil's seeds. That's why we must continually ask God to create in us a clean heart and be sensitive to His prompting to repent and renew our minds.

## Baal and Jezebel Prophets Rising

Understanding Baal worship gives you insight into how Baal prophets operate. *Baal* means "lord" or "possessor." *Baal-Shemaim,* which means "lord of heaven," is his full title. That is clearly false, as there is only one Lord of Heaven and His name is God Almighty. Baal is the sun god of Phoenicia and the supreme deity among the Canaanites and various other pagan nations, according to *The Dake Annotated Reference Bible*.

Baal prophets take on the characteristics of Baal worshipers in the Bible, including religious prostitution (pimping their gift for money), human sacrifice (making people pay for their lifestyle through offerings based on false prophecies), and the like. Baal is also known as "the lord of wealth and abundance" and is a money-hungry god. Remember, Baal was one of the gods, along with Asherah, that Jezebel served. In Elijah's famous showdown, he did away with both companies of false prophets. But we still need to beware of them today because the same spirits that infiltrated the prophetic movement in Elijah's day have infiltrated the prophetic movement in our day.

While applauding the many pure prophetic voices in our day, Patricia King, author, minister, and TV host, has warned about the rise of Jezebel prophets. Unfortunately, there is no denying that the spirit of Jezebel has already hijacked some segments of the prophetic ministry. Like a terrorist who extorts, swindles, or coerces a pilot at gunpoint, the Jezebel spirit is kidnapping prophets who have unresolved character issues, bitterness, hurts, and wounds and is using them for sinister purposes. I've said it before and I'll keep saying it. King says:

> The Jezebelic prophetic voice has been loudly proclaiming sexual perversion to the masses through media, especially, and many in the Church have

bought into the compromise. Unfortunately, they are eating from the table of idols. Jezebelic prophets also use their authority to control, manipulate, and spiritually abuse. …In this day, Jezebelic prophets like in the days of old will attempt to control others by abusing their prophetic authority to fulfill personal agendas and to allure many believers into the snare of ungodly perversions, just like they did in the days of Elijah.

Beware of false prophetic voices who turn people away from the Lord and approve of or make light of unrighteous conduct. Beware also of false prophetic voices that stir up self-effort and religious performance in order to please God. Beware of the false prophetic voices whose words are threaded with condemnation, shame, blame, fear, and control. The true prophetic voice will call you in love to walk in the beautiful light of Christ by speaking the truth of God, who has called you to be.

…In this hour, there are two prophetic companies being released in this hour: God's prophets and Jezebel's prophets. Which mandate will you serve? Which voice will you obey? And whose prophet will you be? And so let's be prophets of God's love, of His truth, of His ways; let's raise up the truth in this day; let's be true to the word; let's be true to righteous morals, and let's obey the word of God together. It is so glorious.[1]

# Beware the Nebuchadnezzar Spirit

Divination can sound a lot like prophecy. Divination can be highly accurate but come from demon powers. (Think about the girl in Acts 16 with the spirit of divination.) This is why the Bible tells us to test the spirits to see if they are from God (see 1 John 4:1).

I've seen a troubling trend in the prophetic movement—a spirit of divination is masquerading as the Holy Spirit. There's such a fascination with the gifts of the Spirit in this hour—particularly the gifts that know something and the gifts that say something—that many don't stop to consider the spirit behind the words or the motive of the person releasing the impressive prophetic utterance.

Time and time again, I've seen people's jaws literally drop when someone can tell them when their birthday is or their name (or the last four digits of their bank account number—scary!). People will stand for hours watching people operate in prophetic gifts, perhaps hoping they are next to receive a revelation. Sadly, a failure to unknowingly judge the source of the gifts of the Spirit is leading many to idolize diviners instead of the Divine One.

Case in point: I recently saw one prophetic pretender manifest with what looked like King Nebuchadnezzar madness in an online video. He was singing mocking words about curses and vindication with a crazed look in his eyes that grieved my spirit.

The number of people who laughed and cheered him on in the lunacy was not only shocking, it was yet another confirmation of the lack of discernment in the Body of Christ—and how many blindly follow personalities instead of following the Person of the Holy Spirit wholly.

# Who Was Nebuchadnezzar?

Over the past 20 years, I've seen many troubling manifestations of the Nebuchadnezzar spirit—the spirit that was on the king who lost his mind in Daniel 4 after he took the glory that belonged to God:

> *At the end of the twelve months he was walking about the royal palace of Babylon. The king spoke, saying, "Is not this great Babylon, that I have built for a royal dwelling by my mighty power and for the honor of my majesty?"*
>
> *While the word was still in the king's mouth, a voice fell from heaven: "King Nebuchadnezzar, to you it is spoken: the kingdom has departed from you! And they shall drive you from men, and your dwelling shall be with the beasts of the field. They shall make you eat grass like oxen; and seven times shall pass over you, until you know that the Most High rules in the kingdom of men, and gives it to whomever He chooses."*
>
> *That very hour the word was fulfilled concerning Nebuchadnezzar; he was driven from men and ate grass like oxen; his body was wet with the dew of heaven till his hair had grown like eagles' feathers and his nails like birds' claws* (Daniel 4:29-33).

I couldn't put a name to what I was seeing in the prophetic movement until the day I witnessed its full manifestation in that video I mentioned and I heard, "Just like Nebuchadnezzar." Since then, I've seen false deliverance ministers using divination to call out accurate information that brings people to tears but leaves them in a much worse spiritual condition. They come to get set free and walk away more demonized through the diviner's impartation.

## Discerning the Nebuchadnezzar Spirit

Now that I have your attention, let's look at what the Nebuchadnezzar spirit is. In researching what I heard the Holy Spirit say while watching these videos, I found an article from Jane Hamon at Christian International. She explains the name *Nebuchadnezzar* means "the power of the prince Nebo." Nebo is a principality and Nebuchadnezzar's guardian god. Now catch this, Jane writes:

> It comes from the Assyrian word that is related to the Hebrew word "nabi." The word "nabi" means "the far hearing; an inspired prophet; one with intelligence who teaches." CI often uses this word to describe our prophetic ministers, so it is no surprise that we would be harassed by this false prophetic principality Nebo.[2]

Hamon outlines a few things Nebuchadnezzar, led by this false prophetic principality, did in his reign. I've used her points in black and commented underneath.

### 1. Nebuchadnezzar took God's people in Israel captive and carried them away to Babylon, which means confusion.

When you receive or connect to the Nebuchadnezzar diviner, you enter into a form of bondage and confusion. You are believing a lie instead of the truth. Your spiritual senses are dulled and your discernment damaged. It becomes harder to hear from the Lord for yourself so you become more dependent on the Nebuchadnezzar diviner, which is exactly what they want.

## 2. Nebuchadnezzar destroyed the Temple in Jerusalem, the house of the Lord, which represents the corporate Body of Christ. He also destroyed many individuals, whose bodies represent the temple of Holy Spirit.

When you connect with a Nebuchadnezzar spirit it can bring destruction into your life and relationships. A young man connected with this divining spirit and lost his pastorate, lost his house, lost his wife, and appears to have lost his mind, same as Nebuchadnezzar.

## 3. Nebuchadnezzar carried away the palace treasures, which locked up the wealth of God's people.

When you sow into someone operating in the Nebuchadnezzar spirit it can bring you into financial distress or even financial ruin. The Body of Christ must stop supporting false prophetic and false deliverance ministries. It's not good ground and we are forwarding the agenda of diviners in doing so.

## 4. Nebuchadnezzar brought death to the king and nation of Israel, the government, and the people of God.

When you connect with a Nebuchadnezzar spirit, it unlocks death instead of life. We are called to walk a prophetic life. Nebuchadnezzar may seem to speak life-giving words but the source is a spirit that ultimately wants to steal, kill, and destroy you.

Ask the Lord to give you discernment about prophetic ministries and deliverance ministries you connect with. Don't be impressed with accuracy for accuracy's sake. Look at the fruit—not the Facebook fruit with the Gucci shoes and slick graphics—the fruit of the word that is sown into your life.

Fruit can take time to bear out, but discernment should give you a red flag about divination. It didn't take Paul months to discern the girl in Thyatira was operating in a spirit of divination. His spirit was immediately troubled. Spend more time with the Spirit of Holiness than you do listening to other ministers and you'll find yourself sharper in the spirit.

King Nebuchadnezzar finally came to his senses and repented. I hope these Nebuchadnezzar prophets do as well. Pray for the prophetic movement. We're in the midst of a reset and the enemy is sowing perversion.

I don't believe Christianity's false prophets start out as false prophets. I believe they go astray somewhere on the road to Christlikeness. We need prophets and intercessors who hear the Spirit accurately and can stand in the ministries they've been called to with integrity. The good news is there are more who are than who aren't, and even if you have fallen into this ditch you can repent and get back on track. In the next chapter we'll begin looking at some of the potholes that derail this vital ministry.

## NOTE

1. Patricia King, "Two Opposing Company of Prophets Arising," December 27, 2019, https://www.youtube.com/watch?v=ATDhEMjRrw8, time stamps 11:07, 14:38, 18:09.

2. Bill Hamon, "Disarm and Render Powerless the Nebuchadnezzar Spirit," Identity Network, accessed April 2, 2020, https://www.identitynetwork.net/apps/articles/default.asp?articleid=25310&columnid=.

# CHAPTER 6

# BEWARE CHARISMATIC WITCHCRAFT

When I was born again, I didn't know there was such a thing as charismatic witchcraft. I thought all Christians were operating out of the same spirit—the Holy Spirit. I thought we were all on the same team. I thought blind loyalty and submission were the sign of a true disciple because that is what I was taught in the Jezebelic church in which I landed. I spent eight years under the cloud of charismatic witchcraft's intimidation and control. Now, I'm warning the Church against it.

Charismatic witchcraft was around long before anyone used those terms to describe it. Charismatic witchcraft didn't start in the prophetic movement either. Yes, there's witchcraft in the Church. Yes, Christians are practicing charismatic witchcraft. If you ask ten different people for a solid definition of charismatic witchcraft, you'll probably get ten slightly different answers. Let's use the definition of witchcraft as a baseline.

The best definition I've found comes from the late Derek Prince. In his classic book *They Shall Expel Demons*, the deliverance minister and spiritual warfare expert pointed to an unnamed dictionary's definition of witchcraft: "the art or exercise of magical powers, the effect or influence of magical powers, or an alluring or seductive charm or influence."

Have you ever heard someone say, "He's got a magical smile." That's another way of saying, "He's got charisma." Charisma is "a personal magic of leadership arousing special popular loyalty or enthusiasm," according to *Merriam-Webster's* dictionary, and "a special magnetic charm or appeal."[1] In considering both definitions and the personal experiences I've had with being the target of charismatic witchcraft, this is my definition: Charismatic witchcraft is exerting ungodly influence through carnal powers of charisma to seduce someone to think or act according to your will.

Charismatic witchcraft begins as a work of the flesh, but left to run its course this fleshly behavior attracts demon powers. These demon powers work through an individual to manipulate, intimidate, control, and ultimately dominate believers in order to bend their will toward their viewpoint. Charismatic witchcraft is released through tactics such as fear, prophetic flattery, and witchcraft prayers. Charismatic witchcraft practitioners seek their own gain, use sincere people who want to serve God to build their own kingdom, and otherwise use and abuse people for their own purposes.

The Shepherding Movement, also known as the Discipleship Movement, may be the most recognizable memory of charismatic witchcraft that spread like wildfire during the Charismatic movement in the 1970s. In fact, the practice is called charismatic witchcraft because of its rise during this important refreshing. Ironically, Derek

Prince was one of the leaders of the movement. God redeemed the experience and gave him revelation on the evil of these practices.

Although the motive for launching the movement was pure, the Shepherding Movement quickly deteriorated into a cult-like environment in which people could not make personal life decisions, including marriage, house moves, and career choices, without their shepherd's permission. I've known folks who have nervously disappeared into their pastor's office to ask permission to marry another congregant, hoping that their request wasn't denied and their love wasn't dashed. And this wasn't during the Shepherding Movement; this was recent.

Today, this type of charismatic witchcraft manifests as spiritual leaders recruiting volunteers to build their ministries while neglecting to minister to the real needs of hurting people. This is not a new practice. You can find instances in the Bible of spiritual leaders exploiting people to build their kingdoms. In Jeremiah 8, the Lord called out the abuse of prophets and priests, saying, "They dress the wound of my people as though it were not serious" (Jer. 8:11 NIV). The root problems of people in the "church" were treated superficially. The pastor's prominence was more important than the legitimate needs of the congregation.

In such cases, churches become like businesses. The pastor is more like a CEO than a spiritual leader who truly loves the flock. Staff meetings center on marketing initiatives that will bring more people—who will bring more tithes and offerings—into the sanctuary. Church services become about external appearances, but the whitewashed tombs are full of dead men's bones. It's religious at best.

Apostles and prophets are employing and deploying charismatic witchcraft to build mega followings with false operations that many do not discern because they are awe-inspired by an accurate utterance. They work in hype and play and prey on people's emotions to get them to pay. Like me, victims of charismatic witchcraft may not realize they have been bewitched until they fully escape the snare. Charismatic controllers tend to hide behind the guise of spiritual coverings. It takes lovers of truth with spiritual discernment to recognize the sometimes-subtle signs of charismatic witchcraft. And it takes courage to confront it.

It may surprise you to learn that what the world—or even what the Wiccans—call witchcraft is not always one and the same as what the Bible calls witchcraft. For example, when you think of witchcraft, you probably think of black magic or conjuring the dead. Those abominations are covered in the Bible, but that's not the fullness of witchcraft as God teaches us in the Word. There are two types of witchcraft mentioned in the Bible—witchcraft as a work of the flesh and spiritual witchcraft. But the work of the flesh can open you up to demonic powers that reinforce carnal behaviors.

## Sensual, Carnal Witchcraft

The Spirit of God is against witchcraft in whatever form it takes, from divination to magic to rebellion to word curses—to works of the flesh. Paul explained that the flesh lusts against the Spirit and the Spirit against the flesh. What are the works of the flesh? Galatians 5:19-21 lists them: "adultery, fornication, uncleanness, lasciviousness, idolatry, witchcraft, hatred, variance, emulations, wrath, strife, seditions, heresies, envyings, murders, drunkenness, revellings, and such like" (KJV).

Notice that witchcraft is listed right alongside adultery and fornication. Witchcraft is a serious offense in any manifestation. As a work of the flesh, witchcraft violates the First Commandment: "You shall have no other gods before me." The flesh opposes the move of the Spirit and resists all things spiritual. This is a serious struggle because Paul assures us that those who practice witchcraft will not inherit the kingdom of God (see Gal. 5:21).

But there is yet good news. If you walk in the Spirit, you will not fulfill the lusts of the flesh (see Gal. 5:16). How do you discern if you are walking in the Spirit? The fruit of the Spirit is love, joy, peace, longsuffering, kindness, goodness, faithfulness, gentleness, and self-control. When you walk in the Spirit, this fruit manifests. That's the same way you discern if someone else is walking in the Spirit. Remember, a prophet may be walking in a spirit, but is he walking in *the* Spirit?

If you know you are disobeying God in an area, repent of this sin, which God views in the same way as witchcraft, and get back in line with the Spirit. If you are cursing people with your negative words of gossip and death, stop practicing this witchcraft and begin blessing. If you are flowing in fleshly witchcraft, crucify your flesh with its passions and desires. If you live in the spirit, walk in the Spirit—and walk free from the practice of witchcraft. Sometimes you don't discern the witchcraft tactics that fool you because you are, yourself, walking in fleshly witchcraft. Let me say this: If you are walking in carnal witchcraft it's more difficult for you to discern charismatic witchcraft because you have come into some level of agreement with it.

# Rooting Out Rebellion

Practicing witchcraft is a serious sin, and far more Christians are experts at sorcery than you may realize. Remember when King Saul was ordered to utterly destroy the Amalekites and everything they had—man, woman, infant and suckling, ox and sheep, camel and donkey? Saul found victory in battle against Israel's enemy by the grace of God, but failed to obey the voice of God when the dust settled. He spared Agag, the king of the Amalekites, and kept the best of the livestock (see 1 Sam. 15:1-9).

Saul proposed that his intention was to sacrifice the animals to the Lord, but there's no excuse for disobedience. Saul was so stubborn that he at first refused to admit his disobedience. He actually justified his actions. Only after Samuel rebuked Saul did he catch the revelation that obedience is better than sacrifice (see 1 Sam. 15:22). In that rebuke—and in Saul's response—we find one way Christians are practicing a sin that's in the realm of witchcraft—through rebellion that arises when the fear of man is greater than the fear of the Lord. Let's listen in on the exchange:

> *For rebellion is as the sin of witchcraft, and stubbornness is as iniquity and idolatry. Because thou hast rejected the word of the Lord, he hath also rejected thee from being king. And Saul said unto Samuel, I have sinned: for I have transgressed the commandment of the Lord, and thy words: because I feared the people, and obeyed their voice* (1 Samuel 15:23-24 KJV).

Unfortunately, Saul didn't learn his lesson. He continued disobeying God and eventually lost his kingdom. Fear of man was at the root of his rebellion, but rebellion grows from many roots. If you see rebellion operating in your life, find the root and rip it out! You can't discern the devil's witchcraft when you are operating in witchcraft.

Saul goes down in Bible history as a witchcraft practitioner and fits the bill of a charismatic controller. Saul led by fear, intimidation, shame, and manipulation. He was known for jealousy and fits of rage when he didn't get his way. He was rash and presumptuous. He demanded too much of the people around him, operating in paranoia, pride, and control. Saul eventually lost his ability to hear from God and alienated the prophet Samuel and wound up consulting mediums, demonstrating that witchcraft was his god.

You may not see charismatic witchcraft practitioners blatantly operate this way on stage, but if you listen to their words you'll hear subtle hints. They will talk about how accurate they are prophetically and brag about their exploits. This violates Scripture because Proverbs 27:2 says, "Let another man praise you, and not your own mouth; a stranger, and not your own lips." Prophets tapping into charismatic witchcraft will take credit for the success of others, insisting your alignment with them is what led to your breakthrough.

## Charismatic Witchcraft Curses

Prophets who operate in charismatic witchcraft may publicly issue curses against other ministries, complete with timelines. I've seen this more than once. A false prophet insisted another minister, who they used to work with, would see their ministry fall apart in 40 days if they did not come to them in repentance. The curse was empty. That same false prophet cursed another ministry, insisting their ministry would fall apart in 30 days because they left his covering. Thirty days came and went and the ministry not only survived, it is thriving since breaking that toxic alignment.

This type of cursing is part of what I call Jezebel's witchcraft. In Second Kings 9:22, right before the wicked queen's demise, Jehu offered insight into an open door for the Jezebel spirit when he told her son, "What peace, so long as the whoredoms of thy mother Jezebel and her witchcrafts are so many?" (KJV). The spirit of Jezebel is essentially a spirit of seduction that works to escort believers into immorality and idolatry (see Rev. 2:20). And this spirit uses witchcraft against its enemies.

Jezebel's witchcraft was rooted in rebellion, but the type of witchcraft in this verse refers to incantations and spells. In the modern church world, we call them word curses. Jezebel released a word curse against Elijah that carried a spirit of fear when she sent him this message: "So let the gods do to me, and more also, if I make not thy life as the life of one of them by to morrow about this time" (1 Kings 19:2 KJV). He went running for the hills, hid in a cave, slept in a witchcraft fog, and wished he was dead.

In modern times, word curses aren't always so dramatic. When we speak negatively over someone's life—"They will never hold down a job acting like that," "Their marriage is bound to fail the way he treats her," "The doctors said he's going to die in thirty days. Isn't that sad?"—we are agreeing with the enemy's plan and giving power to it with our anointed mouths. The power of death and life are in the tongue (see Prov. 18:21). If you are inadvertently—or purposely—releasing witchcraft over people with the words of your mouth, repent and get your mouth back in line with the Spirit of God. Again, if you are operating in witchcraft, it's hard to discern it when it comes to attack you.

## Hype Is Not the Holy Spirit

Strong preaching that gets us up on our feet is healthy. We all need to be stirred up at times, both in our spirit and in our soul, to rise up a little higher. T.D. Jakes is masterful at the art of preaching and teaching and often the congregation shouts him down because the words coming out of his mouth are resonating with a felt need and giving people hope for today—and tomorrow. So they stand and cheer. But the difference between Jakes and practitioners of charismatic witchcraft is the Holy Spirit's operations are missing from the latter group. The Holy Spirit is not inspiring them.

Practitioners of prophetic witchcraft manufacture revival with hype. It's interesting that the first definition of *hype* in *Merriam-Webster's* dictionary is a slang word for "a narcotics addict."[2] People who fall prey to charismatic witchcraft often find themselves addicted to the hype that drew them in. The second definition of hype means "stimulate, enliven." And the third definition is "put on, deceive." The fourth definition is "deception, publicity." As you can see, not one of these is something that sounds at all like how Christ operated in His ministry. As a matter of fact, these are antichrist operations.

Let's look at each one of these definitions briefly for the sake of discerning it when you see it. One of the Greek words for witchcraft in the Bible is *pharmakeia,* which is tied to narcotics. Hyped-up preaching seeks to stimulate your soul but does not feed your spirit. You walk away from the meeting with goose bumps but no real root in you from a true word of God planted in your heart. If the preacher preached the Word, they usually preached it out of context or twisted it, so you have to know the Word well enough to catch the hype.

Hyper grace is a good example —and hyper grace didn't start in the prophetic movement either. Back in the Latter Rain Movement in the 1940s, they called it "greasy grace."Today, we call it hyper grace because it hypes people up emotionally to believe we are forgiven once and for all at salvation and never have to repent for future sins. The motive behind hype is to get into your emotions, not into your spirit. Charismatic witchcraft practitioners know how to exploit the emotions of people. Advertising and marketing firms exploit our emotions, promising breakthrough weight loss, clear skin, and loving relationships if we use their products. False prophets hype emotions to get you to sow for weight-loss miracles, overnight breakthroughs, and the like. I believe in sowing, but you can't buy a breakthrough.

## Selling Breakthroughs

Selling breakthroughs is something we're used to seeing seedy late night televangelists do, but its' taken on a new twist. Some years back, a newspaper reporter called me to solicit my opinion on an elderly woman's so-called "divinely inspired concoctions." Her little shop of mystic wonderments peddles oils, herbs, sprays, and candles that claim to bring love into your life and even get others to obey your every command. As the reporter described the woman's mixtures, supposedly potent enough to solve any problem known to man, I couldn't help but see mental images of the apostle Paul wrestling the beast at Ephesus. But I digress.

The elderly woman has ten grandchildren, ten great-grandchildren, and a divination sanctum littered with statues and images of various saints. A necklace adorned with charms of the tools each saint works with dangles from her neck, according to the reporter's observations.

On Tuesdays this oldster fills an aluminum pan with alcohol, lights it ablaze, and purports to chant away evil spirits.

An incense-filled pot meant to ward off the day's evil guards the back door of her soothsaying studio. Granny acts as trusted advisor to her customers, who share with her problems both large and small. Then she meditates about the issues for a day before mixing a potion of herbs and oils designed to fix what ails them. For this she charges $75—or more—but she offers a 100 percent guarantee and asserts that she hasn't had an unsatisfied customer yet.

If all that is not troubling enough, here is the clincher. The grandmotherly spiritualist professes a strong sense of faith and belief in the Bible and God. (The question is which Bible and what god?) She admitted that all her knowledge about helping people is "in her head" but alleges it is a gift from above.

So what did I say to the reporter who asked me for my view? I told her what you would say: "No Bible-believing Christian would claim a potion could help someone find and keep love. This is a form of witchcraft, essentially," I argued in the newspaper article. "It's not unlike the tarot card reader who proudly displays an image of Jesus in her front office. This woman is merely merchandising lonely people and using a religious mask to make them more comfortable with her deception."

So here I see a merchandising spirit in operation. I see Jezebel deceiving people, many of whom are probably seeking help for hurts and wounds. I see religion attempting to make divination acceptable in the name of the Lord. I see idolatry. I see divination. I see witchcraft. And the world is not the only place I see it.

As Christians, we are quick to recognize the evil behind the tarot card reader, the aura cleansers, the potion makers—and the diviners with foreign accents who pollute the television airwaves with promises they can't keep (even at $2.99 a minute). It seems utterly ridiculous that anyone would be foolish enough to shell out $75 a pop for bogus advice and pleasant-smelling concoctions, doesn't it? I thought so, too, but apparently this level of deception has spread into the Church.

## Can You Buy a Double Blessing?

I recently heard a radio commercial on a Christian broadcast. A "prophet" was proclaiming a double blessing and the prosperity oil to bring it into manifestation for anybody who would sow $29.95 into his traveling ministry. How is this any different from the potion-making granny? OK, the radio prophet charges less for his concoction, but it still reeks of merchandising.

"Here she goes, slamming false prophets again." I can hear my critics now. Please don't stone me. I am passionate about a pure prophetic because the prophetic represents the voice of God. I would rather not be one of those John the Baptist-style preachers assigned to release hard words. Believe me. I'd rather prophesy puppies and popsicles sometimes. But if Jehovah's prophets don't take a stand against this mess—in the world and in the Church—then who will? That brings me back to the apostle Paul and his wrestling match with the beast at Ephesus.

You remember in Acts 19, a huge ruckus broke out because Paul, as Demetrius the silversmith put it, barged in and discredited those who were manufacturing shrines to the goddess Diana. Demetrius stirred up the whole city against Paul for taking a stand against Jezebel worship. The Bible says there was great confusion after the people, who were worried about losing profits from selling their idolatrous wares, began to cry out in praise of Diana. "Some were yelling one thing, some another. Most of them had no idea what was going on or why they were there" (Acts 19:32 MSG).

We need to know what's going on and why we are here—to take dominion; to invade the kingdoms of this world and make them to become the kingdoms of our Lord and His Christ; to set the captives free; to take the gospel to the uttermost parts of the earth.

With all this in mind, who could disagree with the need to break the deception over God-fearing believers who are being sucked in with ambiguous prophetic words that proclaim "the first 100 people to sow $638 according to Luke 6:38" will get their long-awaited breakthrough? Don't get mad at me now. I'm not the only one who has witnessed these things. I hope that you agree that we need to wrestle this beast in the Church. We need to dispel this merchandising spirit from our midst so people are not hoodwinked into buying idols named "breakthrough." You can't buy a breakthrough, healing, or anything else from the Lord any more than you can buy love in a bottle sold by a great-grandmother in Florida.

If you go to a meeting where something doesn't seem right, it probably isn't. If people try to manipulate you for money, run for the door. If ministers are pushing people down at the altar and standing on top of their "slain" bodies—yes, there is a photo of such a thing on Facebook—from such turn away. God is bringing a Third Great Awakening to America marked by signs, wonders, and miracles. We should expect that if the devil can't stop it—and he can't—he will try to offer a counterfeit move to fleece the sheep hungry for an authentic outpouring.

I am praying for a Hebrew 5:14 reality in the Body of Christ—that believers would have powers of discernment and would be trained to distinguish good from evil through practice. In these last days, we cannot take everything we see at face value. I am not suggesting suspicion. I'm advocating for righteous judgment, prophetic insight, and spiritual perception. I'm pleading with believers to study the Word of God, fellowship with the Spirit of God, and pray without ceasing.

Ultimately, I'm just suggesting we do what the Bible says we should do: "Beloved, do not believe every spirit, but test the spirits to see whether they are from God, because many false prophets have gone out into the world" (1 John 4:1 MEV). You can't read a New Testament epistle without finding a warning about deception. Jesus Himself said, "For false christs and false prophets will rise and show great signs and wonders to deceive, if possible, even the elect" (Matt. 24:24 MEV).

# Witchcraft Prayers and Mind Control

Charismatic witchcraft practitioners want to play God in your life. If they do pray for you, they often pray witchcraft prayers. A witchcraft prayer is when you pray your own will instead of God's will. Witchcraft prayers are not Spirit-led but flesh-led. Witchcraft prayers unleash demon powers to tempt and seduce people to think and do what you want them to think and do.

There are signs you are under a charismatic witchcraft attack. Confusion is a primary sign. Confusion is part of the curse of the law (see Deut. 28:28). God is not the author of confusion (see 1 Cor. 14:33). If you are confused as to whether something is of God, that may be the first sign that it's not. A charismatic witchcraft spell works on your identity—or I should say works against your identity in Christ. You become dependent on the leader rather than God to make decisions.

Advanced charismatic witchcraft prayers and spells work to create soul ties between you and the wicked intercessor so that you will feel connected with them and their ministry. That makes it hard to leave. A soul tie is when your soul is knit with another person's. We see this in Scripture in First Samuel 18:1, "Now when he had finished speaking to Saul, the soul of Jonathan was knit to the soul of David, and Jonathan loved him as his own soul." But witchcraft soul ties are dangerous and can be deadly to your spiritual progress in God.

When charismatic witchcraft prayers are released against you, sickness can attack your body, you can feel worn out all the time even though you are sleeping plenty, your emotions can go haywire for no apparent reason, and you can feel alone and lonely. The good news is you have authority over witchcraft and you can break soul ties by aligning your will with the Lord Jesus Christ, repenting for not discerning the assigment quickly, renouncing the witchcraft and relationship with charismatic witchcraft practitioners.

It's noteworthy that most of the leaders of the Shepherding Movement later renounced what it became. The movement, at its peak, had 150,000 followers who were under fierce control. Bob Mumford, one of the Fort Lauderdale Five who initiated the movement, was on the cover of *Ministry Today* magazine in January 1990. The words on the cover said, "Discipleship was wrong. I repent. I ask forgiveness." Derek Prince, who also repented, said, "I believe we were guilty of the Galatian error: having begun in the Spirit, we quickly degenerated into the flesh."

Let's all pray that the charismatic witchcraft practitioners will come to repentance because the Bible is clear—they will not inherent eternal life if they continue down this path. By contrast, pure prophetic prayer can shift your mind, your heart and your life. In our Prophecy Rooms at Awakening House of Prayer, we have witnessed how pure prophetic operations of the Holy Spirit can be a blessing and reverse the curse!

## NOTES

1. Merriam-Webster, s.v. "Charisma," https://www.merriam-webster .com/dictionary/charisma.
2. Merriam-Webster, s.v. "Hype," https://www.merriam-webster .com/dictionary/hype.

# CHAPTER 7

# SELLING PROPHECY AND OTHER PROPHETIC SCAMS

Every week I get at least a handful of digital requests from precious people all over the world desperately seeking a prophetic word. Some come begging. Others come demanding. Still others come with money in hand to buy a prophecy or dream interpretation.

Seriously, this happens just about every day and more than once on most days. It's an unfortunate symptom of modern-day prophetic ministry—prophetic ministry that has too often taught people to depend on prophets to "go to the throne" and "get a word" for them instead of fulfilling the Ephesians 4:11 mandate to equip the saints.

Don't get me wrong. I'm not at all against personal prophecy. In fact, at Awakening House of Prayer, my church in Fort Lauderdale, Florida, we have Prophecy Rooms every Friday night in both English and Spanish. Personal prophecy—edifying, exhorting, and comforting believers—is vital in this hour.

But prophetic ministry doesn't operate like a gumball machine. You can't put in a quarter—or send an e-mail or Facebook message—and out comes a prophetic word. It just doesn't work that way. Part of this misunderstanding is rooted in the proliferation of what I call the "Internet prophets." Some actually take out Google ads promoting how you can get a personal prophecy from them (even every day). Others promise a prophetic word delivered to your e-mail inbox for about the price of a tank of gas. (Sounds like a cheap car salesman ad or a personal injury attorney billboard, doesn't it?)

When I see this sort of stuff, it grieves me for two reasons. First, the gifts of the Spirit are not for sale. We saw Simon the sorcerer try to buy the ability to lay hands on people and get them filled with the Holy Spirit. And we saw Peter sorely rebuke him for it. In fact, Peter said:

> *Your money perish with you, because you thought that the gift of God could be purchased with money! You have neither part nor portion in this matter, for your heart is not right in the sight of God. Repent therefore of this your wickedness, and pray God if perhaps the thought of your heart may be forgiven you. For I see that you are poisoned by bitterness and bound by iniquity* (Acts 8:20-23).

And let's not forget Elisha's servant Gehazi. After Elisha helped Naaman find a cure for leprosy, the commander of the Syrian king's army offered him a gift for his service. Elisha refused, even when Naaman urged him to take it. Gehazi ran after Naaman to collect a reward. Elisha found him out and Gehazi ended up a leper (see 2 Kings 5). I'm not saying that prophets cannot receive offerings for ministry. But we must be careful not to merchandise the gifts of the Spirit. Jesus said, "Heal the sick, cleanse the lepers, raise the dead, cast out demons. Freely you have received, freely give" (Matt. 10:8).

Here's my bottom line: I don't believe in demanding "love offerings" or posting "suggested donation" amounts in exchange personal prophecy. I feel that relegates the prophet to the domain of your local palm reader who charges $5 for a 15-minute session. And I'm not sure the results of such an exchange fare much better for the one seeking supernatural guidance.

# A Baal-Inspired, Jezebelic Practice in the Prophetic

Yes, I've seen people charge for prophetic words many, many times. This spirit of Baal-inspired practice always grieves me, but the latest campaign made my jaw drop to the floor. I left it there to write this article. I will never forget the day I received an e-mail promising me a personal prophetic word every month for just $40 a month. Wow, that's not even the price of a cup of coffee a day! (Seriously, though, imagine how many children we could feed in a Third World country for that investment.)

I was assured receiving a prophetic word from God would help keep me from making so many mistakes and creating setbacks. (I wasn't aware I was making that many mistakes or that I couldn't hear from God myself. This is the power of suggestion at best and taking advantage of desperate, hurting people at worst.) This is also a fear tactic and one of the four pillars of modern-day secular advertising. (The others are guilt, greed, and exclusivity.)

This prophetic merchandiser felt led to send out this email so people who aren't already paying him $40 a month will understand why they should. He highly recommended this subscription so I could hear what the Lord is saying—and even received an endorsement of another well-known prophetic minister, which may have been taken out of context.

By the way, I saw no offer of a money-back guarantee if the word was rotten.

In the same time frame, a young man who is branding himself as a prophet shared with me how he had prophesied over a number of people about starting a business and those businesses were wildly successful. That should have been reward enough, but the young man was complaining that none of them returned with an offering in hand for his ministry. He took credit for their success and wanted a payback. He told me he felt led to start a consulting business to prophesy into people's businesses for a price. This young man went on to enter many aberrant practices and, like Gehazi, has spiritual leprosy. The problem is most people don't discern it and those in his spiritual lineage are coming under the unclean spirit that's covering him.

These examples are Jezebelic. Jezebel calls herself a prophetess but is anything but. In fact, the spirit of Jezebel is a false prophetic spirit that works in divination and smooth sayings to seduce God's people to commit immorality and worship idols (see Rev. 2:20). Far beyond control and manipulation, the spirit of Jezebel works overtime to muzzle—or kill—prophetic voices. If Jezebel's witchcrafts against your mind don't intimidate you, this principality works to pervert the prophetic voice through compromise.

Of course, the Jezebel spirit also works through false prophets—those who set out to deceive—to wring money out of your pocket with sensational prophecies that tap into the idolatry in your heart or fearful prophecies that manipulate the soul.

Knowing these realities shouldn't make you shun prophets or prophetic ministry. God's prophetic movement is like rain on a thirsty Church. When the rain falls, the result is the growth of beautiful grass and flowers—as well as weeds, thorns and thistles. In any garden, there are far more flowers than weeds. Sometimes, you have to eat the hay and spit out the sticks. But you need to know the sticks will choke you or you might try to chew them.

## Why Do People Pay for Prophecy?

Why do so many people give so freely to so many of Jezebel's prophets? Why are some Christians supporting Jezebel's false prophets instead of sowing into the true kingdom of God? Selah. There are a few reasons. One is that they are desperate. Jezebel never uttered a Holy Spirit-inspired prophetic word in her life, but rather she preys on the hurts, wounds, wants, and needs of the soul with divination. But some believers are desperate for supernatural direction—so desperate that they will listen to any voice that says it is of God.

Before I got saved, I used to go to tarot card readers, palm readers, crystal readers—and even call divination hotlines looking for direction for my life. I was going through major trials and I didn't know which way was up—and I didn't know the Lord. I was desperate. Many believers are just as desperate.

Although Jesus clearly said that "My sheep hear My voice. …Yet they will by no means follow a stranger" (John 10:27,5), I've discovered that many believers can clearly hear the voice of the devil telling them to sin, condemning them after they do and otherwise selling them a pack of lies. Many have not been taught that they can hear the voice of God—or trained how to discern and identify the many ways He speaks.

Another reason is they don't understand that prophecy can come from one of three sources—the human spirit, a demonic spirit, or the Holy Spirit—so they don't even attempt to exercise any discernment whatsoever. Our human spirits have plenty of edification, exhortation, and comfort to offer, but that doesn't make our utterances God-breathed prophetic words. On the flip side, demonic spirits are prophesying to many in the Body of Christ through diviners. I'm not talking about the fortune-tellers with the tarot cards and crystal balls in those creepy little shops of horrors. I'm talking about those who prophesy in the name of the Lord (see Matt. 7:22).

Beyond those three sources people can tap into while prophesying, we know that many Internet prophets study the lives of those they are going to prophesy to before releasing a word, or seek information from other means. Some of them peer over the shoulders of victims to catch a glance at the name and address on their offering envelope so they can later prove their prophetic prowess. We know many read body language or otherwise try to "read" their minds.

# Miracle Water, Prayer Soap, and Prosperity Oil

With the rise of Internet prophets, there's a lot of emphasis on selling prophetic words. But believers are still falling for some of the old gimmicks from the 1980s, like miracle water and prayer soap. You can still watch late-night Christian TV shows where they sell this garbage. An investigation of an old-school televangelist revealed the miracle water he was peddling after prime time came from Costco, a mega supermarket. The latest trend is selling Engedi water, which false prophets claim comes from the springs of Engedi in Israel and has supernatural powers. On a recent trip to Israel, I saw this sold for a few sheckles (less than one US dollar) to thirsty tourists. In America, they are selling it for five dollars a bottle and claiming it will bring immediate breakthrough.

New-fangled false prophets have put a new twist on the water miracle gimmick. Some have been pictured spraying miracle water into the eyes of believers who are desperate to see in the spirit but are willing to shortcut the Holy Ghost in order to show off their spiritual senses. Yes, water is found in conjunction with certain miracles in the Bible. Elisha instructed Naaman to dip in the Jordan River seven times to find cleansing from his leprosy in Second Kings, but Elisha refused the commander's financial reward, and when Gehazi chased down Naaman to collect, Elisha pronounced a generational curse over his protégé.

Again, in John 5:4, which some translations of the Bible omit, we see that in a certain season an angel came down to the pool of Bethesda to trouble the water. Whoever got into the water first was healed of whatever disease he had. But there was not anyone standing by with a credit card machine waiting to collect an offering for the experience. In John 9:7, Jesus told a blind man to go wash in the pool of Siloam, and he was healed. But Jesus didn't charge him for a map to find the location of the pool.

False prophets love to use water in their lying signs and wonders (see 2 Thess. 2:9), but it's nothing more than witchcraft. Something called "Florida Water" is used regularly in Santeria. It's used to seek spiritual guidance from ancestors, cleaning altars, as an addition to the ink in a pen with which they write out spells for protection and more. There's a whole category on the dark side called water witches, which work witchcraft with water. I believe water spirits, which I wrote about in my book *The Spiritual Warrior's Guide to Defeating Water Spirits*, are releasing this witchcraft as they are being exalted in these practices.

In 2012, miracle soap claims led to over $25,000 in files for Believe TV.[1] The broadcaster was running testimony programs based on breakthroughs after using Miracle Olive Oil Soap to cure cancer. Nevertheless, Christians are still falling for the miracle soap gimmick. We don't need miracle soap and miracle water. Jesus washes us with the water of the Word (see Eph. 5:26). I'm by no means saying God can't use water in modern-day miracles. But, again, desperation drives people to pay big money for a big nothing. What's next? Jesus spit in mud to heal another man's blindness. Are we going to see containers of spit mud on sale in the false prophet's conference?

When I was very young in the Lord, I was in a meeting—right on the front row—with a prophet whose name you would know if I called it. The anointing was strong. The preaching was good. I was on my feet cheering the prophet on. Suddenly, everything shifted and she started pumping prayer shawls that guaranteed quick prayer answers. She said she only had a few and that whoever was willing to sow $1,000 would be blessed with one of these life-changing prayer shawls. People rushed up with checks in hand to get this "scarce" precious cloth. Little did they know she had a large box full in the back. I ran out of the hotel conference room, through the kitchen, and out into the streets of Philadelphia. That's what you should do when you see a false prophet—grab your purse and run! I asked the Lord, "What happened? When she was preaching, the anointing was tangible." The Lord told me, "When she was preaching My Word, you felt an anointing on the Word. When she started merchandising, I left."

## Don't Put Prophets on a Pedestal

When people come to me seeking, demanding, or offering money for prophetic words it also bothers me because, again, this is often learned behavior. These precious believers genuinely want to hear from God and they don't know it's inappropriate to approach a prophet like a psychic. Again, many saints have been conditioned to run to the prophet every time they need to hear from God. That's not healthy. It puts the prophet up on a pedestal. Every believer can and should be able to hear from God for themselves. Jesus said, "My sheep hear My voice, and I know them, and they follow Me" (John 10:27).

Believers may need training in order to separate the voice of their mind from the voice of the devil from the voice of the Holy Spirit. As I've said repeatedly in the pages of this book, one of the functions of five-fold prophets is to help impart that discernment through practical teaching and training, as well as prayer. But too many prophets—and especially Internet prophets—have set themselves up as the answer man (for a price). In doing so, they are robbing believers of more than money. They are robbing believers of a chance to pursue a more intimate relationship with God.

Again, don't get me wrong. I believe in personal prophecy. And I believe sometimes you need a word from a prophet or prophetic minister as confirmation. There are many voices out there, and when you are under tremendous stress, when you are at a fork in the road and don't know which way to turn, when you have pursued God with all your heart and remain confused—personal prophecy can build you up, offer you direction and warnings, and comfort you.

## Prophetic Ministry Still Misunderstood

So when I get phone calls, e-mails, and Facebook messages begging, demanding, and offering to pay for prophetic words, it grieves me because I can see clearly that there is still a major misunderstanding about prophetic ministry in the Body of Christ. And that can put these precious believers in danger of getting merchandised, deceived, and otherwise steered in the wrong direction in the name of sincerely "seeking God." I don't have time to respond to each and every one in detail about the role of the prophet, why it's inappropriate for prophets to charge for prophecies, or how to hear from God.

But let me assure you of this: God wants to speak to you. In fact, He's probably speaking to you more than you realize. God wants to speak to you directly. Don't run to a prophet—and don't pay a prophet—for prophetic words. Run to God and sow your time into fellowshipping with the Holy Spirit. You won't be disappointed and you won't walk away with a manufactured poor prophecy that leads you in the wrong direction. The Holy Spirit will lead you and guide you into all truth (see John 16:13). That's a promise from King Jesus. Amen.

True five-fold prophets equip the saints for the work of the ministry. They not only declare what God has said and is saying and teach believers how to apply the rhema words they release—they school believers on testing the spirits and inclining their ear to the Lord. Jezebel-inspired prophets profit from this lack of training by making people dependent on them for a word from the Lord rather than pointing them to the One who freely shares words of life.

You can hear from God for yourself. True prophets can confirm what the Lord is saying to you or reveal something new to your heart, but don't be fooled by Jezebel and her witchcrafts (see 2 Kings 9:22). Don't fall into the pay-to-pray trap. Don't buy into the Internet diviner's thievery. Read a book, take an equipping class, or just go hard after God, and you will find the direction you need for your life.

The Bible warns us over and over and over again not to be deceived. We're told the test the spirits (see 1 John 4:1). We must obey the Word and not automatically believe any and every prophecy we hear, even if it comes from someone we admire. Let me add in that we shouldn't have to pay for prayer or prophecies. We must exercise the gift of discernment and know the Word of God, lest we fall prey to false prophets. I pray that the Lord would stir in the heart of every believer a hunger for His Word, for fellowship with His Spirit, and for growth in discernment, in Jesus' name!

## NOTE

1. "Miracle Soap Claims Lead to £25,000 Fine for Religious TV Channel," National Secular Society, February 7, 2012, https://www.secularism.org.uk/news/2012/02/miracle-soap-claims-lead-to-gbp25000-fine-for-religious-tv-channel.

# CHAPTER 8

# THE RISE OF "CHRISTIAN" WITCHES AND PSYCHICS

hile serving as editor at *Charisma* magazine, I received an email from a publicist who aggressively claimed to represent a "devout lifelong Christian" who is also "a clairvoyant, empathic psychic medium and psychic investigator with consultation on more than 100 missing person and cold case files on his resume."

The man claims he communicates with people who have died and is using his gifts to help authorities "solve the unsolvable cases where tracks had run cold." In fact, he calls this his life's work. (Sounds pretty creepy to me.) The trouble with this type of prophetic ministry is that it violates Scripture. I have no doubt he is talking to spirits—familiar spirits who know everything about the deceased person.

Why these familiar spirits would cooperate in solving crimes, I do not know. What I do know is necromancy—which *Merriam-Webster* defines as "conjuration of the spirits of the dead for purposes of magically revealing the future or influencing the course of events"[1]—is an abomination to the Lord. And that didn't change with the New Covenant. Deuteronomy 18:9-13 says:

> When you enter into the land which the Lord your God gives you, you must not learn to practice the abominations of those nations. There must not be found among you anyone who makes his son or his daughter pass through the fire, or who uses divination, or uses witchcraft, or an interpreter of omens, or a sorcerer, or one who casts spells, or a spiritualist, or an occultist, or a necromancer. For all that do these things are an abomination to the Lord, and because of these abominations the Lord your God will drive them out from before you. You must be blameless before the Lord your God (MEV).

That is crystal clear.

The "Christian psychic's" publicist claims he kept his psychic gifts "in the closet," for fear of being ostracized by his Christian community. He counts pastors, Christian authors, and other strict religious devotees as part of his beloved family and insists he's a devout believer. "God gave me this gift. I didn't create it on my own," he says, speaking of his "psychic calling."

Of course, he says, he's accustomed to Christian leaders disagreeing with him—but he is quick to answer that a Christian's job is to love, accept, and preach to all people and not just those who suit the conventional paradigm.

"I take the basic information and then I can pick up on the person and begin to see pictures, places, and things visually in my mind," he says, explaining how he helps investigators. "Going online to Google maps and Google earth helps me put a visual framework to what I am getting in my mind's eye. I can look at an area, pick up clues, and assist in that way."

## Psychic Readings Aren't Prophecy

He apparently does not hesitate to let Christian themes spill over into his "readings." He sees it as a way to comfort and restore faith in clients who are deeply grieving the loss of a loved one.

"Many of the readings I do for private clients are people who have lost children to suicide or to other tragic events, and this has caused them to lose or doubt their faith," he says. "They're looking to repair their faith and my religious background plays a role in helping them on that journey."

This is a tragic deception. The Bible tells us to comfort those who are in any trouble by the comfort with which we ourselves are comforted by God (see 2 Cor. 1:4). That comfort comes from the Holy Spirit.

Christians are not supposed to turn to psychics or prophets to get in touch with dead loved ones. Prophets are not supposed to get prophetic words from any other source but God, yet in this hour we are clearly seeing these and other troubling trends emerge among those who call themselves prophetic. This should not surprise as Paul warned Timothy, "But evil men and seducers will grow worse and worse, deceiving and being deceived" (2 Tim. 3:13 MEV).

He says he is working to change common perception by opening up a public dialogue in the media regarding his "work as a medium and his Christian faith not being in direct conflict, but actually (complementing) one another." With psychic mediums, clairvoyants, and intuitive people coming forward more and more, and their abilities becoming more widely accepted in society, this man feels it is time to address Christianity and psychic phenomena.

"It's a conversation that needs to be had," he says.

Perhaps it is. But it's a conversation that needs to be had with an open Bible.

The Bible says "You shall not eat anything with the blood in it, nor shall you practice divination or fortune-telling" (Lev. 19:26 MEV). The Bible says, "Do not turn to spirits through mediums or necromancers. Do not seek after them to be defiled by them: I am the Lord your God" (Lev. 19:31 MEV). The Bible says, "When they say to you, 'Seek after the mediums and the wizards, who whisper and mutter,' should not a people seek after their God? Should they consult the dead for the living?" (Isa. 8:19 MEV). The Bible says, "The person who turns to spirits through mediums and necromancers in order to whore after them, I will even set My face against that person and will cut him off from among his people" (Lev. 20:6 MEV).

I could go on and on, but we'll stop there. Prophets, can we please do what the Bible says? Christians, please beware of psychics, mediums, familiar spirits, tarot card readers, crystal ball readers, palm readers, and the like. They may claim to serve God, but they are tapping into the spirit realm illegally and offering false comfort and fearful predictions that probably won't even come to pass.

Prophets and psychics can both make accurate predictions. Accuracy is not the only test of a true prophet. Test the spirit behind the word because there are many false prophets making true predictions (see 1 John 4:1).

I posted that on my Facebook page once, and it stirred up a hornet's nest I never would have expected. I thought I'd get a few thousand hearty "amens," open the eyes of some people who had not thought to judge prophecy in this crucial hour, and stir up a few devils. As it turned out, it stirred up more than a few devils who seem to enjoy swimming in impure prophetic pools.

Several people asked me to give Scripture to back up the comment. Of course, the Scripture was listed in the comment. In First John 4:1, John the apostle clearly states by inspiration of the Holy Spirit, "Beloved, do not believe every spirit, but test the spirits to see whether they are from God, because many false prophets have gone out into the world."

## Many False Prophets Are Rising

The backlash against the post caused me to realize just how much confusion there is over prophetic ministry, the source of true prophecy, the function of prophet, and how some will defend soulish prophecy to the death.

As I always say, we wouldn't have to test the spirits if it wasn't for all the false prophets who have gone out into the world. Jesus warned that false christs and false prophets would rise in the end times (see Matt. 24:11). We're seeing that now.

Indeed, I'm seeing blatant misuse of the gift of prophecy. Some who carry the title of prophet have been caught looking over the shoulders of closed-eyed congregants to get an up-close look at their offering envelopes. Later, these prophets give a word to the ones whose envelopes they peeped. Some faithful believers are falling for it hook, line, and sinker.

We're seeing some who call themselves prophets encouraging people to sow $54.17 so they can tap into God's protection promised in Isaiah 54:17, which reads: "No weapon that is formed against you shall prosper, and every tongue that shall rise against you in judgment, you shall condemn. This is the heritage of the servants of the Lord, and their vindication is from Me, says the Lord." Some faithful believers are falling for it hook, line, and sinker. We don't need to pay God for protection like He's a mafia boss—we just need to obey the Lord and believe His Word.

Yes, I'm seeing all manner of foolishness in modern-day prophetic ministry, where prophets are operating in deceptive practices for false profits. Jezebel's puppets are running rampant in the Church. And some faithful believers are not only falling for it hook, line, and sinker to the detriment of their lives and pocketbooks, but they are defending it vehemently.

Remember my original post: "Prophets and psychics can both make accurate predictions. Accuracy is not the only test of a true prophet. Test the spirit behind the word because there are many false prophets making true predictions (1 John 4:1)." Now consider this Scripture:

> On one occasion, as we went to the place of prayer, a servant girl possessed with a spirit of divination met us, who brought her masters much profit by fortune-telling. She followed Paul and us, shouting, "These men are servants of the Most High God, who proclaim to us

*the way of salvation." She did this for many days. But becoming greatly troubled, Paul turned to the spirit and said, "I command you in the name of Jesus Christ to come out of her." And it came out at that moment* (Acts 16:16-18 MEV).

So you see, even someone tapping into a spirit of divination—which the *Interlinear Bible* defines as "to practice divination, divine, observe signs, learn by experience, diligently observe, practice fortunetelling, take as an omen"—can offer an accurate word. Psychics and some false prophets practice divination. They are tapping into a spirit other than the Spirit of God to prophesy.

The woman with the spirit of divination in Acts 16 was correct—she offered an accurate word—but the spirit behind the word troubled Paul. Ultimately, the apostle cast the devil out of her and set her free from this bondage.

It's a dangerous game to knowingly turn to prophets who are operating in a false anointing. Leviticus 20:6 says, "The person who turns to spirits through mediums and necromancers in order to whore after them, I will even set My face against that person and will cut him off from among his people" (MEV).

It's also dangerous to do this unknowingly. The Bible warns us over and over and over again not to be deceived. We're told to test the spirits (see 1 John 4:1). We must obey the Word and not automatically believe any and every prophecy we hear. We must exercise the gift of discernment and know the Word of God, lest we fall prey to false prophets.

# Christian Witches Making Headway in Churches

So-called "Christian" witches love to come to my church, Awakening House of Prayer, in Fort Lauderdale. Mind you, I realize there's no such thing as a Christian witch, but that's what they call themselves.

I've seen a rise of Christians practicing witchcraft. Or maybe they aren't Christians at all. I won't judge someone's salvation, but when people in Church release word curses, pray against you, and conduct unholy fasts to destroy you, the fruit of the Spirit is clearly lacking. Galatians 6 lists both the fruit of the Spirit and the works of the flesh. Witchcraft is among them. But there is a higher level of witchcraft that some so-called Christians are tapping into and it's dangerous.

Christian witches have emerged with a vengeance. Christian witches are targeting government officials like President Donald Trump and Supreme Court Justice Brett Kavanaugh. But they are doing much more behind the scenes and are lifting their voices to recruit the discontented to their campaign.

There are Christians who act like witches and actual Christian witches. Both sides of this prophetic warning were and are true. One example of the latter is Rev. Valerie Love, who has been garnering media attention and ranting on Facebook against anyone who won't accept her as an ambassador of Christ. She wrote on the social media platform:

> Stop thinking you can tell people how to worship.
> Stop thinking you can tell people how to connect with
> the divine. I could tell you how many people have told

me, "You can't be a Christian witch" but here I am. See, you can't tell me how to worship. You cannot tell me how to connect with the divine. That's between me and God. You cannot tell me how to pray.[2]

The late Derek Prince spoke about "Christian witches" many years ago. He espoused there are two kinds of witches. One is people who know they are witches. This is a category of people, like Love, who celebrate their witch-hood and actively release curses, incantations, potions, hexes, vexes, and spells. The second category of Christian witches is those who don't know they are witches—and most other people don't know they are witches, either. These Christian witches may be polite and strong tithers, never missing a church service, but they are operating in witchcraft that control. In charismatic circles, we call this type of Christian witch Jezebel.

Both types of Christian witches are rising in this hour. The first type are in no way part of God's Kingdom. Rather, they are card-carrying members of the kingdom of darkness. The second type may make their way into heaven, but they need deliverance from hurts, wounds, and other issues in their life that make their life a living hell. As a matter of fact, I believe anyone who calls themselves a Christian witch also needs healing and deliverance.

Either way, Jesus died to set these captives free. The Christian witch movement is gaining momentum, but the gates of hell shall not prevail against the Church. Now that this movement has been exposed, let's pray for Christian witches, especially the most vocal ones, to experience a life-changing encounter with the love of the Father that leads them to lay down their sorcery and give testimony to His saving grace.

# Operations of "Christian" Witches and Warlocks

Some "Christian" witches and warlocks are blatant about their beliefs. Others are more subtle in their operations. The Bible shows us what a warlock looks like in the New Testament in Acts 13:6-7:

> *When they had passed through the entire island of Cyprus as far as Paphos, they came upon a certain Jewish wizard or sorcerer, a false prophet named Bar-Jesus. He was closely associated with the proconsul, Sergius Paulus, who was an intelligent and sensible man of sound understanding; he summoned to him Barnabas and Saul and sought to hear the Word of God [concerning salvation in the kingdom of God attained through Christ]* (AMPC).

Let me stop there for a moment. Some Christians are like Sergius Paulus. They look for wisdom in the counsel of many but don't discern some of the many are sorcerers. Like Sergius Paulus, they are intelligent people but they aren't discerning. I know a man who paid a false prophet $10,000 for private mentoring because he was hungry to grow in the things of the Spirit. He got nothing but an empty bank account.

And catch that: His name was Bar-Jesus—many warlocks, sorcerers, and false prophets utter the name *Jesus* from their lips, but the motives are wicked. They practice divination, prophesy accurately out of familiar spirits, and have big bright smiles and wear the latest fashionable clothing. Beware. Another word for warlock is a conjurer or wizard. They claim to practice prophetic arts but they practice magic arts. Not everyone who says Lord, Lord is a true disciple of Christ.

Let's go on to Acts 13:8: "But Elymas the wise man—for that is the translation of his name [which he had given himself]—opposed them, seeking to keep the proconsul from accepting the faith" (AMPC). Notice he had given himself that name. Warlocks, sorcerers, and false prophets give themselves a name. They are not submitted to the name that is above every other name, nor have they been called by the one who holds the name at which every knee must bow and every tongue confess. In other words, Jesus did not call them into the five-fold ministry. These people gave themselves a name and are trying to make a name for themselves.

Acts 13:9 continues: "But Saul, who is also called Paul, filled with and controlled by the Holy Spirit, looked steadily at [Elymas]" (AMPC). Notice how Paul wasn't intimated by the wizardry warlock. He knew his authority. I will not be intimidated by "Christian" warlocks. You have no power or authority over me. Paul was not intimidated and neither should we be.

Let's look at how Paul described him in Acts 13:10:

> *And said, You master in every form of deception and recklessness, unscrupulousness, and wickedness, you son of the devil, you enemy of everything that is upright and good, will you never stop perverting and making crooked the straight paths of the Lord and plotting against His saving purposes?* (AMPC)

You have to understand why Paul was so upset: Elymas was standing in the way of God's will. Nothing makes me more upset than when people purposely thwart God's will.

Paul called him a master of every form of deception, recklessness, unscrupulousness, and wickedness. This is not just someone who practices these things. It's someone who has mastered them. To master something, you have to practice it for a long time. Paul called him a son of the devil, in much the same way Jesus told the Pharisees they were of their father the devil. This is a bold statement. But it's true.

Paul described this warlock as an enemy of everything that is upright and good. Again, a bold statement. They are enemies of God speaking in the name of God. They actively seek to tear down what God is building. That means warlocks are standing against everything that is upright and good and they are enemies of God speaking in the name of God many times. They actively seek to tear down what God is building. Paul said the warlock was perverting *and* making crooked the straight paths of the Lord. Christian witches and warlocks operate in perversion and sabotage. True prophets pave the way for the Lord; they make His path straight. Mark 1:2-3 says, "Look, I am sending My messenger before Your face, who will prepare Your way before You. The voice of one crying in the wilderness: 'Prepare the way of the Lord, make His paths straight'" (MEV). Paul said Elymas was plotting against God's saving purposes. Warlocks want you to go to hell with them. They point you to idols and have you chasing other gods who cannot save.

## NOTES

1. Merriam-Webster, s.v. "Necromancy," https://www.merriam -webster.com/dictionary/necromancy.
2. Valerie Love, Facebook post, September 28, 2018, https://www.facebook.com/ValLove/videos/10212419173224120/ UzpfSTE5MDcxMzkwMTAwNjY0Mjox0DUzNDczMTI0NzMwNzAz.

# CHAPTER 9

# DOCTRINES AND IMPARTATIONS OF DEMONS

D octrines of demons and demonic impartations are mark-
ing some camps in the prophetic movement. Of course,
doctrines of demons have been around since before
Jesus walked the earth and will remain until He returns. It's
a dangerous trend infecting too many innocent believers
who are hungry for a touch from God and spiritually curi-
ous about the mysteries of the Kingdom (see Matt. 13:11).
Thank God for the Word and the Spirit, which warn us about
such doctrines.

What some false prophets and false teachers are calling "mysteries" are actually fueled by a spirit of error. Worse, some of these
"mysteries" are really heresies. Because of the word famine in the
United States in particular, we're seeing believers buy into these
errors, heresies, and doctrines of demons. What we're seeing is
something I prophesied in 2015:

*"A tsunami of perversion and all manner of wicked sin is headed toward this nation. You've only yet seen the rumblings of what the enemy has planned. For many in your nation have called good evil and called evil good. Many in this nation have not believed you will reap what you sow.*

*"You have sown iniquity—for decades—and you have taken the hand of perversion. You have walked in step with abominations rather than resisting the temptations to deny My Word and My Son. The perversion in this land will increase and increase and increase.*

*"There will come a day when morality is no longer merely relative but is persecuted. There will come a day when evil is considered good and good is considered evil. When that day comes, those who are hidden in the shadow of My wings will be insulated from the abominations around them.*

*"I will raise up the likes of Abraham and Moses to deliver the righteous out of the hand of the wicked in that day. I will shield those who run into My Name. But no longer look and no longer think that you will turn the tide by your prayers alone. These things must be so. I warn you now to fear not, but to ready your hearts. Buy your oil. Be ready for My coming."*

Yes, we've seen the rumblings of this rising perversion, but I believe it's going to grow darker still. When you think of perversion you probably immediately think of sexual perversion—and I believe that's part of it. But it became clear to me that the root of this tsunami of perversion is actually the perversion of God's Word itself. We're seeing prominent pastors and entire denominations perverting God's Word, twisting it to defend and justify perversion itself, and suggesting the rest of us are legalistic or unenlightened about the truth. Peter warned:

> But there were also false prophets among the people, even as there will be false teachers among you, who will secretly bring in destructive heresies, even denying the Lord who bought them, and bring on themselves swift destruction. And many will follow their destructive ways, because of whom the way of truth will be blasphemed. By covetousness they will exploit you with deceptive words; for a long time their judgment has not been idle, and their destruction does not slumber (2 Peter 2:1-3).

## What Are Doctrines of Demons?

You've heard the Bible speak of doctrines of demons. Paul uses this phraseology in First Timothy 4:1-2: "Now the Spirit expressly says that in latter times some will depart from the faith, giving heed to deceiving spirits and doctrines of demons, speaking lies in hypocrisy, having their own conscience seared with a hot iron."

We're certainly seeing many depart from the faith in recent years. For every famous Christian who makes Christian media headlines for renouncing Christ, know that many more have walked away whom we've never heard of. Yes, the *great falling away* Paul and Jesus prophesied is beginning before our very eyes, which is a clear sign that doctrines of demons have infiltrated the Church—even the prophetic movement.

Revelation 2, which speaks of Jezebel the false prophetess in Thyatira, offers some telling truth in connection with Paul's prophecy. Revelation 2:24 promises: "Now to you I say, and to the rest in Thyatira, as many as do not have this doctrine, who have not known the depths of Satan, as they say, I will put on you no other burden." The depths of satan is a particular dimension of the doctrines of demons. Satan is the prince of demons.

The New International Version calls these "Satan's so-called deep secrets." The New Living Translation refers to them as "depths of Satan." And *The Passion Translation* calls them "deep satanic secrets." Again, what some false prophets and false teachers are calling mysteries are actually fueled by a spirit of error. And some of these "mysteries" are really heresies—or even the deep secrets of satan. Before you get too impressed with a "deep" message you've never heard before, judge the source. Satan comes as an angel of light with deep revelation that leads some away from Christ.

We've witnessed more than one man of God with a major ministry platform bow a knee to doctrines like universalism, deceiving and being deceived with this deadly heresy. Despite many in the Church lifting their voices against heretical teachings, these deceived ministers hold fast to their demonic doctrines. Clearly, the conscience of some prophets and other church leaders has already been seared with a hot iron (see 1 Tim. 4:2). Some have become the proverbial blind leading the blind—and they are all falling into a deadly ditch (see Luke 6:39). Paul wrote:

> *But know this, that in the last days perilous times will come: For men will be lovers of themselves, lovers of money, boasters, proud, blasphemers, disobedient to*

*parents, unthankful, unholy, unloving, unforgiving, slanderers, without self-control, brutal, despisers of good, traitors, headstrong, haughty, lovers of pleasure rather than lovers of God, having a form of godliness but denying its power. And from such people turn away!* (2 Timothy 3:1-5)

Paul's laundry list of idolatrous ingrates is not particularly new, but the love of many has certainly grown colder. Many prophets (and other ministers) ignore the homeless (and the widows and the orphans). All the while, they spend multiplied thousands on sermon props and video announcements that rival MTV so they can entertain an idolatrous generation on Sunday mornings with a user-friendly message that waters down the gospel. Some pastors offer a 20-minute sermonette and afterward neglect the opportunity to lay hands on the sick, get people filled with the Holy Spirit, or otherwise open up the altar for believers seeking a touch from God. This form of godliness does not make room for God's power. Pleasure has taken its place.

And many believers are eating it up and sowing mega bucks into these ministries while true leaders are suffering lack. Paul warned in Second Timothy 4:3-4:

*For the time will come when they will not endure sound doctrine, but according to their own desires, because they have itching ears, they will heap up for themselves teachers; and they will turn their ears away from the truth, and be turned aside to fables.*

We see some of this among congregations even now. Beyond universalism, there's the prosperity gospel that only demonstrates one side of the cross. There's the grace message that perverts the gospel. These are fables. Billy Graham once filled stadiums with his bold preaching on subjects like hell and holiness. Today, seeker-friendly preachers fill stadiums to hear a motivational message followed by a call to give. Many modern believers may cringe if they had to endure a Billy Graham sermon on hell. Again, some deny the existence of hell.

Paul warned: "Beware lest anyone cheat you through philosophy and empty deceit, according to the tradition of men, according to the basic principles of the world, and not according to Christ" (Col. 2:8). It's up to you not to be deceived. Jesus warned, "Many false prophets will rise up and deceive many."

Victorious believers will overcome satan by the blood of the Lamb and the word of their testimony—and the fact that they did not love their lives even unto death (see Rev. 12:11). I fear there may be fewer victorious believers at the end of the age than some may think. The Bible tells us to work out our salvation with fear and trembling (see Phil. 2:12). We need to get at it because this is sure: Jesus is coming back for a glorious Church without spot or wrinkle (see Eph. 5:27). I believe the spots and wrinkles will fall away before His return. The gates of hell are trying to prevail against the Church and will ultimately fail, but not before enticing some believers into heresy, idolatry, and other sin.

I don't believe in once-saved, always-saved doctrines. I believe you can lose your salvation. I don't think it happens overnight. I think it's a slow progression down the slippery slope of deception. I often ask people who are deceived this question: "How would you know if you were deceived?" I've never met one who was deceived find an answer for the question. Rather, they insist that they cannot be deceived or that they would know if they were. If we don't think we could be deceived, we're deceived already. And if we are deceived, we wouldn't know it unless the Holy Spirit broke in and opened the eyes of our heart. Paul wrote:

> *If anyone teaches otherwise and does not consent to wholesome words, even the words of our Lord Jesus Christ, and to the doctrine which accords with godliness, he is proud, knowing nothing, but is obsessed with disputes and arguments over words, from which come envy, strife, reviling, evil suspicions, useless wranglings of men of corrupt minds and destitute of the truth, who suppose that godliness is a means of gain. From such withdraw yourself* (1 Timothy 6:3-5).

## Demonic Impartations

Impartations can be godly or demonic. Impartation is both a scriptural concept and a spiritual reality. Impartation is a divine transfer that releases an ability you didn't have before. Through impartation, the Holy Spirit gives or grants you a spiritual gift, revelation, or power that you need to fulfill your purpose. Paul told the church in Rome:

> *For I am yearning to see you, that I may impart and share with you some spiritual gift to strengthen and establish you; that is, that we may be mutually strengthened and encouraged and comforted by each other's faith, both yours and mine* (Romans 1:11-12 AMPC).

*Impart* in this context simply means "impart" or "give." It means to grant as from a store. God has a great storehouse of gifts and He wants to impart what will strengthen you in your calling. *Young's Literal Bible* translates this "to give a share of." We can receive impartation from God Himself or from anointed men and women through the laying on of hands, through applying oil, by sitting under a teaching anointing (which is why it's so dangerous to sit under erroneous teaching), or directly from God.

Genesis 28:1-4 reveals we can receive blessings through impartation:

> *Then Isaac called Jacob and blessed him. Then he charged him and said to him, "You must not take a wife of the daughters of Canaan. Arise, go to Paddan Aram to the house of Bethuel your mother's father, and take for yourself a wife from there, from the daughters of Laban your mother's brother. May God Almighty bless you and make you fruitful and multiply you, so that you may become a multitude of people. May He give you the blessing of Abraham, to you and your descendants with you, that you may inherit the land where you are a stranger, which God gave to Abraham"* (MEV).

If you can receive a blessing through impartation of laying on of hands, doesn't it make sense you can receive a curse? The enemy is looking for a point of contact. I have known on-fire Christians who came in contact with witches who took a strand of their hair and they wound up with bald spots and blemishes all over their body. Be careful who you allow to lay hands on you.

Acts 8:14-17 shows how we can receive an impartation of the Holy Spirit through the laying on of hands:

> *Now when the apostles who were at Jerusalem heard that Samaria had received the word of God, they sent Peter and John to them. When they came down, they prayed for them that they might receive the Holy Spirit, for still He had come on none of them. They were only baptized in the name of the Lord Jesus. Then they laid their hands on them, and they received the Holy Spirit* (MEV).

If we can receive the Holy Spirit through laying on of hands, don't you think we can receive some other spirit—a demonic spirit—through the laying on of hands? Be careful who you allow to lay hands on you.

First Timothy 4:14 shows how we can receive spiritual gifts by the laying on of hands: "Do not neglect the gift that is in you, which was given to you by prophecy, with the laying on of hands by the elders" (MEV). If we can receive Holy Spirit gifts through prophecy and the laying on of hands, don't you think we can receive divination and false anointings through the laying on of hands? Be careful who you allow to lay hands on you.

Luke 4:40 demonstrates how we can receive healing through the laying on of hands: "Now when the sun was setting, all those who had anyone sick with various diseases brought them to Him. And He laid His hands on every one of them and healed them." If we can receive healing through a point of contact, don't you think we can receive the spirit of infirmity through a point of contact? Be careful who you allow to lay hands on you.

# Can Spirits Really Transfer?

Yes, demon spirits really can transfer from one person to another. You can't catch a demon the way you would catch a cold or flu, but you can walk into a meeting completely free and walk out demonized and not even know it. Although we have authority over demons, when we enter into situations where the Holy Spirit did not lead and allow a demonized person to lay hands on us or spray miracle water into our eyes, we have given permission for demons to enter.

And, again, willfully sitting under someone who is teaching by the influence of the spirit of error can open you up to a spirit of error. I have been warned not to sit under the teaching of certain leaders in the Body of Christ because they are walking in heresy and a spirit of error marks their ministry. Although much of their teaching is good, that spirit of error is still lurking. The Bible actually speaks of the spirit of error in First John 4:6: "We are of God. He who knows God hears us; he who is not of God does not hear us. By this we know the spirit of truth and the spirit of error."

I have also been warned not to associate or align with certain leaders for the same reason. We are not to be unequally yoked (see 2 Cor. 6:14). While this Scripture is generally spoken over people who want to marry or start business partnerships with unbelievers, you can also be unequally yoked with believers. You can receive demonic impartations through error you read in books, amulets people give you, and other ways. The reality is clear: Demons can transfer from one person to another in many ways. Be careful who you let lay hands on you.

# CHAPTER 10

# WHAT SPIRIT ARE YOU OF?

There's a deluge of prophecy in the Body of Christ. Never before have so many people stepped out to prophesy. Modern technology, especially social media, is making it easier than ever before to release a prophetic word to the masses. It's a tremendous opportunity for edification, exhortation, and comfort. But it's also a tremendous opportunity for the enemy to make error "go viral"—and in some cases it has.

In two separate instances in Scripture, Jesus flat-out rebuked His disciples for allowing other spirits to influence them. The word *rebuke* is actually used in both Luke 9:55 and Matthew 16. *Rebuke* is a strong word. The Greek word for rebuke is *epitiamao*. According to *The King James New Testament Greek Lexicon*, it means "to adjudge, award, in the sense of merited penalty; to tax with fault, rate, chide, rebuke, censure severely; to admonish or charge sharply." *Merriam-Webster*'s dictionary defines *rebuke* as "an expression of strong disapproval, reprimand, to criticize sharply."[1] A rebuke is much stronger than a correction.

Peter received the first rebuke, and James and John received the second. Peter's encounter with Jesus demonstrates how someone can be inspired by the Spirit of God in one instance and inspired by satan in the next. It's startling when you think about it in this way. We see the instance in Matthew 16:13-23:

> When Jesus came into the region of Caesarea Philippi, He asked His disciples, saying, "Who do men say that I, the Son of Man, am?" So they said, "Some say John the Baptist, some Elijah, and others Jeremiah or one of the prophets." He said to them, "But who do you say that I am?" Simon Peter answered and said, "You are the Christ, the Son of the living God."

> Jesus answered and said to him, "Blessed are you, Simon Bar-Jonah, for flesh and blood has not revealed this to you, but My Father who is in heaven. And I also say to you that you are Peter, and on this rock I will build My church, and the gates of Hades shall not prevail against it. And I will give you the keys of the kingdom of heaven, and whatever you bind on earth will be bound in heaven, and whatever you loose on earth will be loosed in heaven." Then He commanded His disciples that they should tell no one that He was Jesus the Christ.

> From that time Jesus began to show to His disciples that He must go to Jerusalem, and suffer many things from the elders and chief priests and scribes, and be killed, and be raised the third day. Then Peter took Him aside and began to rebuke Him, saying, "Far be it from You, Lord; this shall not happen to You!" But He turned

*and said to Peter, "Get behind Me, Satan! You are an offense to Me, for you are not mindful of the things of God, but the things of men."*

# Get Behind Me, Satan!

One minute, Peter was receiving revelation directly from the Father. Jesus called him blessed. The next moment, Peter allowed his own desires to get in the way of God's will. This offers us a key to how we open ourselves up to being influenced by some other spirit and offend God. Jesus called Peter *satan*. He didn't turn in his direction to speak to satan. He said it directly to Peter. Peter was under the influence of satan in that moment. He took his mind off the things of God and put it on the things of men and it opened the door to another spirit. In that moment, he did not know what spirit he was operating in.

The New Living Translation translates the words of Christ this way: "Get away from me, Satan! You are a dangerous trap to me. You are seeing things merely from a human point of view, not from God's." *The Passion Translation says*, "Jesus turned to Peter and said, 'Get out of my way, you Satan! You are an offense to me, because your thoughts are only filled with man's viewpoints and not with the ways of God.'"

Judas had the same issue. Judas was offended over the way Jesus was handing the ministry finances, so he betrayed Him for money—30 pieces of silver to be exact. Judas was among the 12 handpicked apostles of the Lamb. He had cast out devils with the best of them. Now, suddenly, he was acting like the devil. He was more interested in money than souls. Luke 22:3-6 reveals:

*Then Satan entered Judas, surnamed Iscariot, who was numbered among the twelve. So he went his way and conferred with the chief priests and captains, how he might betray Him to them. And they were glad, and agreed to give him money. So he promised and sought opportunity to betray Him to them in the absence of the multitude.*

Scripture doesn't say a garden-variety demon entered him, but satan himself. Stop and think about that. Clearly, Judas did not know what spirit he was of in that moment. I believe people get offended with God for a variety of reasons. John the Baptist was offended with Jesus because he found himself in prison. John actually sent his disciples to ask the Lord if He was really the Christ. Some ministers get offended because others who seem less spiritual are promoted before they are, and they unknowingly invite familiar spirits into their lives. Offense truly is the bait of satan and it's destroying prophetic destinies. I heard the Lord say:

*"A spirit of offense is rising and running rampant through the Church. Those who are easily offended are candidates for the Great Falling Away. Those who cultivate and maintain an unoffendable heart will escape many of the assignments the enemy will launch in the days to come.*

*"For My people must band together in this hour and refuse to allow petty arguments and soulish imaginations to separate them. This is the time to press into community and relationship and reject the demonic notions and wisdom the enemy is pouring out.*

> *"The love of many is waxing cold. Brother is turning against brother and sister against sister—in My Body. You must come to the unity of the faith in order to accomplish what I've called you to do in this hour. The time is upon you. The opportunity is before you. Lay aside the resentment, bitterness, and unforgiveness and, as far as it depends upon you, seek peace with all men.*
>
> *"Humble yourselves even among those whom you feel are your enemies and I will work to bring reconciliation that sets the scene for unity from which the anointing flows. You need My anointing to combat the antichrist spirits rising in this hour.*
>
> *"Many of My people are wrestling in their flesh, engaging in works of the flesh, and otherwise letting the flesh lead in battle—and they are battling flesh instead of the spirits influencing the flesh. This is the result of offense. Forgive, let go, embrace your brothers and sisters despite their flaws and sins. I have."*

## Operating in the Wrong Spirit

Jesus didn't rebuke Peter and John when they wanted reserved seating at His right and left hand in eternity. He knew that was just immaturity. But when the sons of thunder wanted to call down fire from heaven on a Samaritan village because they were offended, Jesus issued a strong rebuke. We see the account in Luke 9:51-56:

> *Now it came to pass, when the time had come for Him to be received up, that He steadfastly set His face to go to*

*Jerusalem, and sent messengers before His face. And as they went, they entered a village of the Samaritans, to prepare for Him. But they did not receive Him, because His face was set for the journey to Jerusalem. And when His disciples James and John saw this, they said, "Lord, do You want us to command fire to come down from heaven and consume them, just as Elijah did?" But He turned and rebuked them, and said, "You do not know what manner of spirit you are of. For the Son of Man did not come to destroy men's lives but to save them." And they went to another village.*

The Amplified Bible, Classic Edition translates Luke 9:55 like this: "He turned and rebuked and severely censured them. He said, You do not know of what sort of spirit you are." The New Heart English Bible offers a troubling translation: "You do not realize what kind of Spirit you belong to." The disciples took on offense for Christ's behalf—and Christ was certainly not offended—and tapped into the wrong spirit. That spirit was the very spirit that caused satan to rebel against God—pride. Pride comes before destruction. Knowledge puffs up (see 1 Cor. 8:1).

The *Geneva Study Bible* offers this on Luke 9:55: "So speak the Hebrews, that is, you know not what will, mind, and counsel you are of: so the gifts of God are called the spirit, because they are given of God's Spirit, and so are they, that are contrary to them, which proceed of the wicked spirit, as the spirit of covetousness, of pride, and madness."[2]

*Matthew Henry's Commentary* on this verse reads: "Above all, they were ignorant of the prevailing motives of their own hearts, which were pride and carnal ambition. Of this our Lord warned them."[3] We need to check our heart motives regularly. Jeremiah 17:9 tells us, *"The heart is deceitful above all things, and desperately wicked; who can know it?"* We know that out of the abundance of our heart, our mouth speaks. So we need to live a lifestyle of repentance, dealing with our biases, offenses, and pride to avoid moving in the wrong spirit.

## Familiar Spirit or the Spirit of Prophecy?

Bringing this conversation into the context of divination and prophecy, I have noticed that "prophetic people" who operate in a familiar spirit have pinpoint accuracy in some matters, but when the familiar spirit is not helping them they miss it terribly. In other words, when they don't rely on demons, they aren't accurate.

One false prophet prophesied to me that I should return as editor of *Charisma* magazine. I knew that wasn't of the Lord. Not only did God lead me to leave when I did, it was confirmed by several leading prophets. This same false prophet prophesied that someone in his network should move to a larger building, then went around bragging that because of his anointing their church went from fifty to four hundred. It was all a lie. By the time the young man realized the prophet was manipulating him, he was paying two rents and looking at a largely empty church every week.

The deception is when these false prophets are moving in divination they are scary accurate. They can prophesy names, addresses, bank account numbers, and the like. They know things about you that no one else knows but you, God, and perhaps your parents or spouse. Familiar spirits are at work but it seems like the Holy Spirit because the information is so obscure and private. False prophets often rely, either knowingly or unknowingly, on monitoring spirits.

Monitoring spirits are spirits that monitor you. *Merriam-Webster*'s dictionary defines *monitor* as "to watch, keep track of, or check usually for a special purpose."[4] Monitoring spirits are spiritual peeping toms and evil eavesdroppers. They are satanic watchdogs. They are illegal informants. They are part of a demonic network that watches and reports information back to higher-ranking demonic powers so they can devise plans to steal, kill, and destroy you. False ministers tap into these spirits, which work in the realm of divination and witchcraft. I teach more about this in my School of the Seers because monitoring spirits like to lure seers to tap into visions illegally.

The devil can't be everywhere all the time, so monitoring spirits are dispatched to follow you, listen to your conversations, watch your reactions to situations, determine who you are close to and what you care about most. Monitoring spirits are like the devil's private investigators. You can't see them, but they can see and hear you. The devil is not omnipresent or omniscient, so he depends on monitoring spirits to gather information.

Monitoring spirits are called by many names, including familiar spirits, masquerading spirits, ancestral spirits, fowlers (see Ps. 124:6-7), besiegers (see Jer. 4:16), spirit spies, demonic messengers, and watchers. We know there are watcher angels in the Bible, mentioned three times in Daniel 4. The enemy counterfeits what God does, and monitoring spirits are active in the false prophetic and deliverance movement.

Some of these false ministers actually believe they are work-ing with angels, but they are actually cooperating with angels of darkness in disguise. In Second Corinthians 11:13-15, Paul was speaking about false apostles, but the same holds true for any false minister:

> *For such are false apostles, deceitful workers, transform-ing themselves into apostles of Christ. And no wonder! For Satan himself transforms himself into an angel of light. Therefore it is no great thing if his ministers also transform themselves into ministers of righteousness, whose end will be according to their works.*

Paul nailed it when he wrote, "But evil men and impos-tors will grow worse and worse, deceiving and being deceived" (2 Tim. 3:13).

## Paul Confronts the Familiar Spirit

Paul discerned and confronted a familiar spirit working in a slave girl in Thyatira. Some translations call it a spirit of divination, or a spirit by which she predicted the future, or a spirit of clair-voyance, or a spirit of python, or a spirit of prediction, or an evil spirit that told fortunes. This is the same spirit that is informing some prophetic ministries today. Acts 16:16-19 gives the account:

> *Now it happened, as we went to prayer, that a certain slave girl possessed with a spirit of divination met us, who brought her masters much profit by fortune-telling. This girl followed Paul and us, and cried out, saying, "These men are the servants of the Most High God, who*

*proclaim to us the way of salvation." And this she did
for many days. But Paul, greatly annoyed, turned and
said to the spirit, "I command you in the name of Jesus
Christ to come out of her." And he came out that very
hour. But when her masters saw that their hope of profit
was gone, they seized Paul and Silas and dragged them
into the marketplace to the authorities.*

Paul discerned it because it annoyed or troubled his spirit.
When you come in contact with prophecy emanating from a
familiar spirit, it should trouble your spirit. Just because a word
is accurate doesn't mean God is the source. Remember what Jesus
said in Matthew 7:21-23:

*Not everyone who says to Me, "Lord, Lord," shall enter
the kingdom of heaven, but he who does the will of My
Father in heaven. Many will say to Me in that day,
"Lord, Lord, have we not prophesied in Your name,
cast out demons in Your name, and done many wonders
in Your name?" And then I will declare to them, "I
never knew you; depart from Me, you who practice
lawlessness!"*

So what are we going to do with that? Jesus undeniably calls
out those who prophesy, cast out devils, and do mighty works.
He is obviously talking about prophetic ministry in these verses
(not that they don't apply to anyone else). Jesus began His teaching with a warning about false prophets and then drilled down to
the core issue of some of these false prophets—self-will.

Let's look at this verse again in light of some of the translations of the Greek words. *Prophesied* translates as "exercised the

prophetic office." *Name* translates as "authority." *Wonderful works* translates as "miracles." *Knew* translates as "allowed." And *iniquity* translates as "lawlessness." So the Scripture could read this way: "Many will say to me in that day, Lord, Lord, have we not *exercised the prophetic office* by your *authority*? And by your *authority* cast out devils? And by your *authority* done many *miracles?* And then will I profess unto them, I never *allowed* you: depart from me, ye that work *lawlessness*" (see Matt. 7:22-23 KJV).

In other words, "You did not do the will of My Father. You did your own will. You were self-willed. You did what you wanted to do without asking God what He thought about it. You prophesied without permission. You cast out devils to draw attention to yourself. You used your gifts, which are without repentance, as it pleased you. You may have used My name, but I didn't call you to do those things."

## God Condemns Familiar Spirits

God warns against consulting with familiar spirits—and that would include prophets who operate in familiar spirits. Leviticus 19:31: *"Give no regard to mediums and familiar spirits; do not seek after them, to be defiled by them: I am the Lord your God."* King Manasseh was deemed evil in the sight of the Lord because he relied on familiar spirits and wizards (see 2 Kings 21:6).

God condemns familiar spirits over and over again in the Bible. In Leviticus 20:6 God says, *"And the person who turns to mediums and familiar spirits, to prostitute himself with them, I will set My face against that person and cut him off from his people."* Revelation 22:15 reveals people who operate in familiar spirits will not enter

---

heaven: "But outside are dogs and sorcerers and sexually immoral and murderers and idolaters, and whoever loves and practices a lie." These warnings are not to be ignored.

The "depart from me" verse should strike the fear of the Lord in us and cause us to examine what spirit we are of. False ministers don't take the time to examine themselves, which is vital to working out our salvation with fear and trembling (see Phil. 2:12). Anyone can fall into deception at any time.

Paul wrote, "For if we would judge ourselves, we would not be judged" (1 Cor. 11:31). Paul also wrote, "Examine yourselves as to whether you are in the faith. Test yourselves. Do you not know yourselves, that Jesus Christ is in you?—unless indeed you are disqualified" (2 Cor. 13:5). *The Message* says, "Test yourselves to make sure you are solid in the faith. Don't drift along taking everything for granted. Give yourselves regular checkups. You need firsthand evidence, not mere hearsay, that Jesus Christ is in you. Test it out. If you fail the test, do something about it."

Many believers who love the Lord with all their heart, all their mind, all their soul, and all their strength are misplacing their hopes on flattery from false prophets, sowing into false prophetic ministries, and sharing their false prophetic utterances on social media, thereby spreading the deception. We won't go to hell for believing a false prophecy, but we may see spiritual attacks in our lives and miss God's perfect will for our lives if we allow ourselves to be deceived.

Remember this: You are your own best prophet, and Christ in you is not only the hope of glory but the voice of exhortation, edification and comfort. Get trained how to hear God's voice, spend time in His Word and test the spirits in your personal life. Then you'll be able to discern familiar spirits operating through others.

## Notes

1. Merriam-Webster, s.v. "Rebuke," https://www.merriam-webster .com/dictionary/rebuke.

2. *Geneva Study Bible* (Peabody, MA: Hendrickson Publishers, 2007), Luke 9, footnote y.

3. *Matthew Henry's Commentary*, Luke 9:55, https://biblehub.com/ commentaries/luke/9-55.htm.

4. Merriam-Webster, s.v. "Monitor," https://www.merriam-webster .com/dictionary/monitor.

# CHAPTER 11

# CAN SATAN CAST OUT SATAN?

I've been casting out devils for decades, but recently the Holy Spirit has led me to put a stronger emphasis on deliverance ministry. I am encouraged because I see a new breed of deliverance ministers rising, but I am simultaneously seeing the enemy sowing tares among the wheat (see Matt. 13:25).

I'm grateful for the pioneering work Derek Prince, Lester Sumrall, and others did in the realm of deliverance ministry. And I'm equally grateful for modern-day deliverance ministers like Alexander Pagani, because many pastors still won't touch the issue of casting out demons.

In a move to encourage the new breed of deliverance ministers and demystify deliverance, I launched a School of Deliverance and have pressed into more mass deliverance events at Awakening House of Prayer. While on a Facebook Live about reasons more pastors don't embrace deliverance ministry, right at the end of the broadcast I had an unction to prophesy. I heard the Lord say:

*"I am raising up even now, in your midst, a new generation and a new breed of deliverance ministers. And they will be bold like lions. They will not shrink back nor will they be intimidated by the tactics of the enemy. For I am putting new mantles on my deliverance ministers who are willing to take the tough cases, who are willing to go where others will not venture.*

*"And I am going to give them new revelations and new flows of My anointing. New rivers will flow out of them as I pour My anointing into them. And they will see even clearly inside bodies what is going on, where the stronghold is. They will see the names of the demons even written in the spirit, like the handwriting that was written on the wall in the days of Daniel.*

*"And they will cooperate one with another; they will become companies of deliverance ministers who will run together. They will share intelligence, and they will cooperate with one another for My glory. For there will not be a strong competition in the realm of deliverance as we see even now in the realm of the apostolic and in the realm of the prophetic, because these ministers have set themselves apart and they understand the need for clean hands and a pure heart.*

*"So they will celebrate with one another and celebrate each other and they will relish the victories over the kingdom of darkness together. And they will network together, not in the sense of building their own king-*

*dom, but in order to share the stories of glory from My Spirit in the realm of deliverance.*

*"I am doing a new thing in deliverance ministry. Have you not yet heard about it? Well, I am announcing it to you even now in a bold way. Begin to watch and begin to pray. But also, know and recognize that many will come and try to take this new mantle—this new time and season of deliverance ministers rising up—as a fad and a trend. And they will try to hook their wagon to the greater wagon and try to use the momentum of the tide and the flow that I am bringing to the Body of Christ.*

*"But, they will not carry the authority because their heart is compromised. They will not carry the authority that the pure ones do because they are not in it for the right reasons, and they will end up like the sons of Sceva because I don't know these ones—not the way that I need to know them—because they kept part of their heart back from Me. And watch as the false deliverers arise, needing deliverance themselves. And you will see and know that I will sweep through the Body of Christ and I will do a new thing in deliverance ministry in this hour."*

## False Deliverance Ministers Rising

The first part of that prophecy is super encouraging. The last several sentences are super alarming. The Lord spoke to me about this before I saw the depth of it, and over the course of the following months He made sure I got a firsthand look at some of the shenanigans going on in the Body of Christ.

Yes, false deliverance ministers are rising and reinforcing some pastors' beliefs that they should shy away from this vital aspect of Christ's ministry. This is nothing more than an enemy ploy to keep people in bondage or put them in worse bondage through demonic encounters under the guise of casting out demons. We know this: satan can't cast out satan. Those aren't my words. They are the words of the Deliverer Himself, Jesus Christ. Consider the account in Matthew 12:22-30:

> *Then one was brought to Him who was demon-possessed, blind and mute; and He healed him, so that the blind and mute man both spoke and saw. And all the multitudes were amazed and said, "Could this be the Son of David?" Now when the Pharisees heard it they said, "This fellow does not cast out demons except by Beelzebub, the ruler of the demons."*

> *But Jesus knew their thoughts, and said to them: "Every kingdom divided against itself is brought to desolation, and every city or house divided against itself will not stand. If Satan casts out Satan, he is divided against himself. How then will his kingdom stand? And if I cast out demons by Beelzebub, by whom do your sons cast them out? Therefore they shall be your judges. But if I cast out demons by the Spirit of God, surely the kingdom of God has come upon you. Or how can one enter a strong man's house and plunder his goods, unless he first binds the strong man? And then he will plunder his house. He who is not with Me is against Me, and he who does not gather with Me scatters abroad."*

# Satan Can't Cast Out Satan

Catch that. Jesus said, "If Satan casts out Satan, he is divided against himself. How then will his kingdom stand?" (Matt. 12:26). The New Living Translation puts it this way: "And if Satan is casting out Satan, he is divided and fighting against himself. His own kingdom will not survive." *The Message* says bluntly: "If Satan banishes Satan, is there any Satan left?" Finally, *The Passion Translation* asserts, "So if Satan casts out Satan, he is making war on himself. How then could his kingdom survive?" *Matthew Poole's Commentary* offers some keen insight on this verse:

> The sum of the argument is: The devil is so wise, that he will look to the upholding of his own kingdom in the world. This will require an agreement of the devils amongst themselves, for if they be divided they cannot uphold their kingdom, nor stand, any more than a house, city, or kingdom in the world so divided can stand; therefore the prince of devils will not forcibly cast out the inferior devils.[1]

The devil is not stupid. He won't cast his minions out of their host homes because demons need bodies to work through.

But Poole doesn't stop there. He drives home an important point that few seem to understand when they leave the safety of their pastor and run in desperation to a flashy, YouTube-driven deliverance minister who promises quick-fix freedom without ever mentioning the name of Jesus. Poole writes about those who run to a deceived deliverance minister who works for the devil hoping to get free from the devil:

There is but one imaginable objection to this: Do we not see the contrary to this in people's going to cunning men for help against those that are bewitched, to get help for them? And is there no truth in those many stories we have of persons that have found help against the devil for some that have traded with the devil? I answer, It is one thing for the devils to play one with another, another thing for them to cast out one another. One devil may yield and give place to another, to gain a greater advantage for the whole society, but one never quarrels with another.

...When a poor wretched creature goeth to one who dealeth with the devil for help for one who is vexed with some effect of the devil, one devil here doth but yield and give place to another by compact, voluntarily, and for the devil's greater advantage; for it is more advantage to the devil (who seeks nothing so much as a divine homage) to gain the faith of one soul, than to exercise a power to afflict many bodies. In such cases as these, the devil, for the abatement of a little bodily pain, gains a power over the soul of him or her who cometh to implore his help, and exerciseth a faith in him. This is an establishing, promoting, and enlarging his kingdom.[2]

One might understand why oppressed souls visit a witch doctor in a primitive society where the gospel is not preached. One could fathom why diseased people would visit a shaman to find a cure for an ailment that plagues them when there is no medical doctor in sight in a Third World nation. One might even under-stand how desperate people could land in the hands of a false deliverance minister because their pastor won't help cast out their demons. But this practice leaves people worse off than they were.

At Awakening House of Prayer, one of our members' sisters was visiting the region for the holidays. Somehow, she landed in the camp of a false deliverance minister hoping to find freedom from trauma. This deliverance minister wore all white with red, which is how Santeria witches dress. (Santeria is big in South Florida due to our large Cuban population.) She didn't discern the Santeria connection. She didn't notice the deliverance minis-ter wasn't using the name of Jesus. She didn't get delivered either. She walked away more oppressed and my team had to minister to her the next day.

Here's what happens in these encounters. Because satan can't cast out satan, the deliverance minister is actually imparting a spirit that's more powerful (yes, demons have rankings) than the demon that they came in complaining about. The person at first feels relief, because the more powerful demon is hiding in their soul, subduing the demon that they discerned. But after some time, they will have more issues than they had before because the more powerful demon will begin its ministry to steal, kill, and destroy their life.

## What About Lying Signs and Wonders?

Satan uses lying signs and wonders—a counterfeit anointing—to win the attention of people who are desperate for miracles. The devil is flashy and convincing if you lack discernment. The Bible warns about lying signs and wonders. We see several instances of lying signs and wonders in the Book of Revelation, the end of the end times. In Revelation 13:11,13-14, John:

> *Saw another beast coming up out of the earth.… He performs great signs, so that he even makes fire come down from heaven on the earth in the sight of men. And he deceives those who dwell on the earth by those signs which he was granted to do in the sight of the beast, telling those who dwell on the earth to make an image to the beast who was wounded by the sword and lived.*

And in Revelation 16:13-14, John:

> *Saw three unclean spirits like frogs coming out of the mouth of the dragon, out of the mouth of the beast, and out of the mouth of the false prophet. For they are spirits of demons, performing signs, which go out to the kings of the earth and of the whole world, to gather them to the battle of that great day of God Almighty.*

In relation to the end times Jesus prophesied, "For false christs and false prophets will rise and show great signs and wonders to deceive, if possible, even the elect. See, I have told you beforehand" (Matt. 24:24-25). And over 2,000 years ago Paul said:

> *For the mystery of lawlessness is already at work; only He who now restrains will do so until He is taken out of the way. And then the lawless one will be revealed, whom the Lord will consume with the breath of His mouth and destroy with the brightness of His coming. The coming*

*of the lawless one is according to the working of Satan,
with all power, signs, and lying wonders, and with all
unrighteous deception among those who perish, because
they did not receive the love of the truth, that they might
be saved* (2 Thessalonians 2:7-10).

Let that sink in. They did not receive the love of the truth.
*The Passion Translation* puts it even more strongly: "because they
rejected the love of the truth." *The Message* puts it perhaps even
more strongly: "they refuse to trust truth." And, if possible, the
Amplified Bible, Classic Edition translation takes it up even
another notch: "they did not welcome the Truth but refused to
love it that they might be saved."

One problem with discernment is people love themselves and
cater to self more than to God. They love themselves more than
the truth. This is also part of the reason why false ministers are rising so rapidly. Paul expounded on this in Second Timothy 3:1-4:

*But understand this, that in the last days will come (set
in) perilous times of great stress and trouble [hard to
deal with and hard to bear]. For people will be lovers
of self and [utterly] self-centered, lovers of money and
aroused by an inordinate [greedy] desire for wealth,
proud and arrogant and contemptuous boasters. They
will be abusive (blasphemous, scoffing), disobedient to
parents, ungrateful, unholy and profane. [They will be]
without natural [human] affection (callous and inhu-
man), relentless (admitting of no truce or appeasement);
[they will be] slanderers (false accusers, troublemak-
ers), intemperate and loose in morals and conduct,*

*uncontrolled and fierce, haters of good. [They will be] treacherous [betrayers], rash, [and] inflated with self-conceit. [They will be] lovers of sensual pleasures and vain amusements more than and rather than lovers of God* (AMPC).

Remember what Jesus said in Matthew 7:21-23:

*Not everyone who says to Me, "Lord, Lord," shall enter the kingdom of heaven, but he who does the will of My Father in heaven. Many will say to Me in that day, "Lord, Lord, have we not prophesied in Your name, cast out demons in Your name, and done many wonders in Your name?" And then I will declare to them, "I never knew you; depart from Me, you who practice lawlessness!"*

*The Message* puts it this way:

*Knowing the correct password—saying "Master, Master," for instance—isn't going to get you anywhere with me. What is required is serious obedience—doing what my Father wills. I can see it now—at the Final Judgment thousands strutting up to me and saying, "Master, we preached the Message, we bashed the demons, our God-sponsored projects had everyone talking." And do you know what I am going to say? "You missed the boat. All you did was use me to make yourselves important. You don't impress me one bit. You're out of here."*

# Signs of False Deliverance Ministers

So how do you recognize false deliverance ministers? I can't give you an exhaustive list. It's important that you use discernment and not limit your test to the few issues I share here. In essence, you can revert back to the signs of false prophets and many of them will also apply to false deliverance ministers. But here are a few more:

## *Make a Show Out of Deliverance*

False deliverance ministers make a big show out of deliverance. They are flashy. They are not exalting Christ but exalting themselves. They have extended conversations with demons, calling them up and binding the manifestations as if it's some kind of game of demonic hide and seek.

## *Do Not Respect the Privacy of the Client*

False deliverance ministers do not respect the privacy of those they are ministering to. YouTube is proof of that. You will find horrifying videos of deliverance ministers imparting demons while a camera is right up in the face of the client on one side and a microphone is right under their chin on the other side so that the audience can hear demons talking and screeching. I can understand showing deliverance videos for educational purposes, but this would mean obscuring the identity of the one who is being delivered.

## *Charging for Deliverance Ministry*

There is nothing wrong with receiving love offerings, as it takes money to do ministry. Some deliverance ministries also charge a small administrative fee for processing applications. It does cost money to hire administrators. But false deliverance ministers will charge many hundreds of dollars for a private session. I saw one who charges $1,000 an hour.

### Use Your Deliverance to Promote Their Ministry

False deliverance ministers will use the client's weakest, most vulnerable moments to promote their own ministry. They do this through Facebook clips and other social media. The motive is not to educate. The motive is to demonstrate how powerful they are and why you should pay them to cast out your devils.

### Purposely Prey on Desperate People

When people are desperate, they are open to deception—and false deliverance ministers know this. "O foolish Galatians! Who has bewitched you that you should not obey the truth, before whose eyes Jesus Christ was clearly portrayed among you as crucified?" (Gal. 3:1). Jesus is our Deliverer, and although He uses people to cast out devils, if a deliverance ministry is not Christ-centered they are not working for Christ.

### Sell Products to Help You Maintain Your Deliverance

False deliverance ministers sometimes try to add to the work of Christ. Some sell amulets and miracle water, bracelets, oil, and sprays. You don't need anything but the Word of God and the Spirit of God to walk out your deliverance.

### NOTES

1. Matthew Poole's Commentary, Matthew 12:26, https://biblehub.com/commentaries/matthew/12-26.htm.
2. Ibid.

# CHAPTER 12

# A PROPHETIC
# SHOWDOWN COMING

> *"Just like Elijah confronted the prophets of Baal, the time is coming when God's New Testament mouthpieces will confront modern-day merchandisers. The true will defy the false. The holy will challenge the unholy. Until that day, spirits of divination, with a little help from the lust of the eyes, the lust of the flesh, and the pride of life, are working overtime to woo God's true prophets to the side of error."*

I wrote those words in 2001 and I can prophesy this now: We are closer to the showdown today. Much closer.

Throughout the pages of this book, you've read my bold confrontations of false prophets. I've called out many dangers and how to discern them. Perhaps the most dangerous merchandisers are those who use their gift to tap into divination. These prophets announce what the believer wants to hear in order to sow a false seed of faith in his heart and reap an improper financial reward, inappropriately earned position, or wrongly received recognition. No matter the merchandiser's brand of deceit, it is a practice that stinks in the nostrils of God.

> *Then the Lord said, "These prophets are telling lies in my name. I did not send them or tell them to speak. I did not give them any messages. They prophesy of visions and revelations they have never seen or heard. They speak foolishness made up in their own lying hearts. Therefore, this is what the Lord says: I will punish these lying prophets, for they have spoken in my name even though I never sent them. They say that no war or famine will come, but they themselves will die by war and famine!"*
> (Jeremiah 14:14-15 NLT)

## The First Prophetic Showdown

Prophetic showdowns are part of Bible history and I believe there will be more major showdown before Christ returns. The first prophetic showdowns took place not long after the creation of man. We find the account in Exodus 7:8-13 when God was preparing to deliver His people Israel from the bondage of a cruel Egyptian system:

> *Then the Lord spoke to Moses and Aaron, saying, "When Pharaoh speaks to you, saying, 'Show a miracle for yourselves,' then you shall say to Aaron, 'Take your rod and cast it before Pharaoh, and let it become a serpent.'" So Moses and Aaron went in to Pharaoh, and they did so,*

*just as the Lord commanded. And Aaron cast down his rod before Pharaoh and before his servants, and it became a serpent.*

*But Pharaoh also called the wise men and the sorcerers; so the magicians of Egypt, they also did in like manner with their enchantments. For every man threw down his rod, and they became serpents. But Aaron's rod swallowed up their rods. And Pharaoh's heart grew hard, and he did not heed them, as the Lord had said.*

Some believers' hearts have been hardened against God. They will defend the false prophets and diviners because they see power working through them, but it's not the power of the Holy Spirit. They are fierce and harsh in opposing anyone who questions the false prophets' motives. Here's what has happened: Because they idolize a man, putting him before God, they become like an idol themselves.

*They have mouths, but they do not speak; eyes they have, but they do not see; they have ears, but they do not hear; noses they have, but they do not smell; they have hands, but they do not handle; feet they have, but they do not walk; nor do they mutter through their throat. Those who make them are like them; so is everyone who trusts in them* (Psalm 115:5-8).

Put another way, their spiritual senses are dulled. They can't see the deception. They can't hear the lies. They can't smell the stench God smells. They can't discern it. They did not exercise their spiritual senses to discern between good and evil (see Heb.

5:14). They did not test the spirits. Now they are serving those spirits with their time and money and are accomplices to the crime.

To Israel and Egypt, it looked like the magicians had the same power as Moses. In Exodus 8:7, the magicians were able to bring frogs forth just like Moses did. In Exodus 8:18, the magicians were able to bring forth lice just like Moses did. By Exodus 8:19, even the magicians were convinced that Moses was operating under a higher power and tried to convince Pharaoh to stand down—but he refused.

## The Second Prophetic Showdown

Some years later, Elijah called for a prophetic showdown with the prophets of Baal on Mount Carmel. His motive, and my motive, was to turn the hearts of God's people away from the false and back to the one true living God. Read the account in First Kings 18:20-40 and really let this sink in:

> So Ahab sent for all the children of Israel, and gathered the prophets together on Mount Carmel. And Elijah came to all the people, and said, 'How long will you falter between two opinions? If the Lord is God, follow Him; but if Baal, follow him.' But the people answered him not a word. Then Elijah said to the people, "I alone am left a prophet of the Lord; but Baal's prophets are four hundred and fifty men. Therefore let them give us two bulls; and let them choose one bull for themselves, cut it in pieces, and lay it on the wood, but put no fire under it; and I will prepare the other bull, and lay it on the wood, but put no fire under it. Then you call on

*the name of your gods, and I will call on the name of the Lord; and the God who answers by fire, He is God."*

*So all the people answered and said, "It is well spoken." Now Elijah said to the prophets of Baal, "Choose one bull for yourselves and prepare it first, for you are many; and call on the name of your god, but put no fire under it."*

*So they took the bull which was given them, and they prepared it, and called on the name of Baal from morning even till noon, saying, "O Baal, hear us!" But there was no voice; no one answered. Then they leaped about the altar which they had made.*

*And so it was, at noon, that Elijah mocked them and said, "Cry aloud, for he is a god; either he is meditating, or he is busy, or he is on a journey, or perhaps he is sleeping and must be awakened." So they cried aloud, and cut themselves, as was their custom, with knives and lances, until the blood gushed out on them. And when midday was past, they prophesied until the time of the offering of the evening sacrifice. But there was no voice; no one answered, no one paid attention.*

*Then Elijah said to all the people, "Come near to me." So all the people came near to him. And he repaired the altar of the Lord that was broken down. And Elijah took twelve stones, according to the number of the tribes of the sons of Jacob, to whom the word of the Lord had come, saying, "Israel shall be your name." Then with the stones he built an altar in the name of the Lord; and he made a trench around the altar large enough to hold two seahs of seed. And he put the wood in order, cut the bull in pieces, and laid it on the wood, and said, "Fill four waterpots with water, and pour it on the burnt sacrifice and on the wood." Then he said, "Do it a second time," and they did it a second time; and he said, "Do it a third time," and they did it a third time. So the water ran all around the altar; and he also filled the trench with water.*

*And it came to pass, at the time of the offering of the evening sacrifice, that Elijah the prophet came near and said, "Lord God of Abraham, Isaac, and Israel, let it be known this day that You are God in Israel and I am Your servant, and that I have done all these things at Your word. Hear me, O Lord, hear me, that this people may know that You are the Lord God, and that You have turned their hearts back to You again."*

*Then the fire of the Lord fell and consumed the burnt sacrifice, and the wood and the stones and the dust, and it licked up the water that was in the trench. Now when all the people saw it, they fell on their faces; and they said, "The Lord, He is God! The Lord, He is God!" And Elijah said to them, "Seize the prophets of Baal! Do not let one of them escape!" So they seized them; and Elijah brought them down to the Brook Kishon and executed them there.*

## Don't Be Afraid of the Showdown

Certainly, we won't see these exact same scenes in the next prophetic showdown, but I do believe it will have elements of drama.

The point is this: the power of these diviners does not match the divine power that is in us. Elijah made sure that the power of God was evident by stacking all the odds against himself. He drenched the altar with water, but the fire of God still licked it all up.

Beyond these showdowns, we see repeatedly that the wisdom and power from diviners does not match the wisdom and power of God. In Genesis 41:15, the Bible reveals that Pharaoh in Joseph's day could not find anyone to interpret his dreams. Despite all the magicians in the land, Pharaoh could not get an answer. Joseph interpreted the dream by the revelation of God. Again in Daniel's day, Nebuchadnezzar could not find anyone to interpret his dream either. He called in all the magicians and astrologers and sorcerers but they came up empty. In fact, they said there was no man on earth who could give the king an interpretation. But Daniel not only interpreted the dream, he told the king what his dream was before launching into God's interpretation (see Dan. 2).

So how do you deal with a diviner when you meet one? Most of the time, the best thing to do is withdraw yourself from the meeting. If you are aligned or connected in any way with a false prophet, disconnect. Block them from your social media and your phone so they have no access. Break soul ties if they were formed. You also need to repent before the Lord if you spread their false prophetic propaganda. Ephesians 5:11 is clear: *"And have no fellowship with the unfruitful works of darkness, but rather expose them."*

Should you really expose them or mark them? Romans 16:17 says, "Now I urge you, brethren, note those who cause divisions and offenses, contrary to the doctrine which you learned, and avoid them." You have to be led by the Holy Spirit. I believe you should let the people you run with know so they can avoid the same mistake you made, or share your discernment in cases where you've avoided entanglement. But should you name them publicly?

Sometimes, you have to. Sometimes, I have. Most of the time I have not because people will take that list of names and throw discernment out the window thinking anyone who is not on the list is safe. I prefer to teach the principles so people can discern, but I have called out names in the past and will again. You have to be led by the Spirit.

For example, who were the men who "crept in unnoticed, who long ago were marked out for this condemnation, ungodly men, who turn the grace of our God into lewdness," whom Jude talked about in his letter to the Church (Jude 4)? Who were the ones Jude pronounced woe on—the ones who went the way of Cain, ran greedily in the error of Balaam for profit, and perished in the rebellion of Korah (see Jude 11)? Who were the "spots" in the love feasts (see Jude 12)?

You can't tell me because Jude never named them.

What about the false teachers Peter pointed out? He called these depraved false teachers "spots and blemishes" who were "carousing in their own deceptions," having "eyes full of adultery and that cannot cease from sin, enticing unstable souls." He called them out for having "hearts trained in covetous practices." He called them accursed children (see 2 Pet. 2:13-14). He marked them as those who "have forsaken the right way and gone astray, following the way of Balaam the son of Beor, who loved the wages of unrighteousness" (2 Pet. 2:15). And he called them out for promising liberty when they themselves were "slaves of corruption" (2 Pet. 2:19).

Tell me, who were they? You can't tell me because Peter never named them.

And let's not forget the false apostles Paul pegged. He called these false apostles "deceitful workers, transforming themselves into apostles of Christ." And then he dared to say that it was no wonder, since satan himself transforms into an angel of light. Paul went on to say that it's no great thing if satan's ministers, these false apostles, "also transform themselves into ministers of righteousness, whose end will be according to their works" (2 Cor. 11:13-15).

Tell me, who were they? You can't tell me because Paul never named them.

There is a time to name names and there is a time not to name names. Paul named Phygellus and Hermogenes as ones who turned away from him (see 2 Tim. 1:15). He also named Demas, who forsook him because he "loved this present world" (2 Tim. 4:10). But keep in mind that this was a personal letter warning his spiritual son rather than a letter to the entire Body of Christ warning of false gospels.

John named Diotrephes in a letter to the local church at Gaius. He said:

> *Diotrephes, who loves to have the preeminence among them, does not receive us. Therefore, if I come, I will call to mind his deeds which he does, prating against us with malicious words. And not content with that, he himself does not receive the brethren, and forbids those who wish to, putting them out of the church* (3 John 1:9-10).

But keep in mind that John did this from a disciplinary stance in that single church body, not as a warning to the universal Church about false gospels.

Jesus issued warning after warning about false prophets and false teachers and false christs and wrong doctrine. We don't know the names of the ones He was warning about. He often shared the principles these false ones taught, but He didn't always. For example, Jesus didn't tell us what doctrines the false christs and false prophets who will rise and show signs and wonders to deceive would be propagating (see Mark 13:22). He told us so we could be ready and discerning.

When Jesus pronounced woe on the scribes, Pharisees, and hypocrites, He explained why they were worthy of woe, but He didn't follow up His list of woes with a list of names (see Matt. 23). He clearly outlined the reasons for the woes, but that doesn't automatically paint every Pharisee with the brush of guilt.

Jesus called out satan by name, but He wasn't in the habit of calling out specific people. I believe that's because satan is the one influencing the false prophets and false teachers and false christs and wrong doctrine. We're not wrestling against flesh and blood but "against principalities, against powers, against the rulers of the darkness of this age, against spiritual hosts of wickedness in the heavenly places" (Eph. 6:12).

So, why did those who scribed the Bible choose to name names sometimes and not other times? Could it be possible they were led by the Holy Spirit? If the Scripture is Spirit-inspired, and it is, then these men were led at times to name names and at other times not to name names.

The same holds true today. I've named names and been criticized for it. I've declined to name names and been criticized for it. I've named names and been thanked for it. Makes no difference to me. I'm not here to win man's approval. I've been delivered from the man-pleasing spirit.

It's the fear of the Lord that drives me to write these warnings. I'm staying true to my prophetic calling. These warnings coming through my pen—and the pens of many others—are not what is bringing division to the body. Rather, the people preaching error (or not living right) are causing the controversy. When we expose the error, we are pointing people back to Jesus and toward true unity.

I refuse to stand by and watch this cancer grow in the body and then turn a blind eye as many are led astray. I refuse to whitewash a false gospel in the name of unity. That's called compromise, and there's a price to pay for taking that route. I'm willing to pay the price for standing for truth. I don't want to pay the price for compromising God's calling on my life. Do you? Amen.

I believe there will be a more public showdown with false prophets and true prophets. The confrontation in the pages of this book hopes to spur some of them to repentance before we get to the power displays.

## Every Prophet Is Tempted

Don't think you or your leader is above falling. Again, most false prophets don't start their ministries as false prophets; rather, they are tempted and enticed by the idolatry in their hearts. Avoiding satan's snare begins with the fear of the Lord and the promised wisdom that follows. After all, the merchandise of wisdom is better than the merchandise of silver, and the gain thereof than fine gold. Wisdom is more precious than rubies, and all the things that you can desire are not to be compared to her (see Prov. 3:14-15).

Balaam is best remembered for his talking donkey. He was a true prophet of God who went the way of divination for the promise of financial gain when King Balak offered him rewards to curse Israel. But Balaam did not fall into sin upon the first temptation. In fact, he refused the king's initial offer. His royal majesty then upped the ante, promising the prophet promotion, honor, and power if he would curse the Israelites. Balaam once again refused, saying, "If Balak would give me his house full of silver and gold, I cannot go beyond the word of the Lord my God, to do less or more" (Num. 22:18 AMPC).

Despite his bold confession to obey the Lord's will, Balaam secretly desired to attain the rewards pledged by the king. And so the testing begins. Balaam would follow his rebellious heart 320 miles on a donkey's back to curse Israel and claim his coveted merchandise. But to his surprise, the Lord would not allow him to pronounce the curse when he arrived in Moab. Disappointed and still hoping to collect the king's bribe, Balaam shared a strategy to trip up the Israelites through sexual sin that led to the downfall of his brethren.

Balaam had a clear way of escape: Telling the king's messengers upon their first visit that the Lord forbade him to curse Israel. That would have closed the door to future offers and put an end to the temptation that would lead to his destruction. The end of Balaam came by the command of Moses at the sword of his own people—the Israelites he tried to curse through divination.

Daniel, on the other hand, refused to give in to the temptation presented in King Belshazzar's dilemma. Belshazzar and his guests were drinking from gold and silver cups that his father had stolen from God's temple and giving praises to idols when the fingers of a human hand appeared and wrote on the palace wall. Belshazzar was frightened and summoned enchanters, fortune-tellers, and diviners to come, promising riches and power to anyone who could interpret it. When none could, the king called Daniel and made him the same offer (see Dan. 5).

Daniel was faced with at least three choices at this critical turning point in his ministry. He could accept the king's offer to interpret the message, thereby merchandising his gifting. He could exercise the gift he had freely received from Jehovah to freely interpret the message, all the while knowing that such a harsh word from the Lord could land him in the lion's den. Or he could stand on his credible reputation as God's prophet to falsely interpret the warning message as a blessing message and in all likelihood collect the loot anyway.

Unlike Balaam, Daniel unlocked the hard truth in the writing on the wall. He told the king that his days were numbered and that his kingdom would be divided up and handed over to the enemies. Daniel refused to compromise, no matter the consequences, and God used the king to promote him. As one of his last acts as king, Belshazzar robed him in purple, draped a great gold chain around his neck, and positioned him as third in charge of the entire kingdom.

King Ahab and his wife Jezebel took the tradition of kings calling on prophets to unlock the mysteries of god a step further—and a few steps too far. Jezebel had false prophets on her payroll.

The wicked queen regularly fed 450 prophets of Baal and 400 prophets of Asherah. Bible scholars estimate that feeding those false prophets cost her about $12,750 a week or $663,000 a year. That's a hefty price tag for a good prophetic word.

So while Jezebel's prophets had full bellies in a time of famine, the queen cut off the prophets of the Lord for fear of the truth (see 1 Kings 18:4). Obadiah, a type of religious spirit, hid 100 of God's prophets in caves and fed them bread and water. While this may appear like a good work on the surface, Obadiah was only facilitating Jezebel's plan to cut off the uncompromising prophetic word.

While Jezebel's prophets looked well-fed and God's true prophets looked like sheep being led to the slaughter, the story changes in a hurry when Elijah confronts the 850 merchandisers at Mount Carmel in what goes down in biblical history as the ultimate showdown between the true and the false. Elijah threw down the prophetic gauntlet and challenged the false camp to bring fire down from heaven by calling upon their god. The merchandising diviners cried to Baal from dawn to dusk with no answer.

When the false camp had finally exhausted itself, Elijah built an altar holding a sacrifice to Jehovah, drenched it with four barrels of water, said a simple prayer, and watched as the fire of God fell from heaven and consumed the sacrifice, the wood, the stones, the dust and even the water in the trench. Then Elijah slew his false counterparts one by one. So the ultimate fate of the false prophets came at the hand of the true prophet, who was later taken to heaven in a chariot of fire.

Like Old Testament prophets, modern-day prophets are also being tempted to merchandise the anointing for fame, fortune, or friends in high places. Being plugged into a strong local apostolic church is a safety net because apostles boldly confront false moves of the Spirit and give merchandisers a way of escape by leading them into deep repentance.

Recall Simon the sorcerer, who was highly esteemed among the Samarians because he bewitched them. The apostles Peter and John met up with Simon after praying for the baptism of the Holy Ghost for the new believers there. When Simon saw that the people were filled with the Spirit when the apostles laid their hands on them, he offered them money:

> *Saying, Give me also this power, that on whomsoever I lay hands, he may receive the Holy Ghost. But Peter said unto him, Thy money perish with thee, because thou hast thought that the gift of God may be purchased with money. Thou hast neither part nor lot in this matter: for thy heart is not right in the sight of God* (Acts 8:19-21 KJV).

Simon may have repented and did ask the apostles to pray for him. Repentance is the appropriate response for New Testament prophets who fall into the trap of merchandising.

There's a group of prophets in a Facebook group who self-identify as generals. Most of the prophecies on the page are about money, payback, recompense, and breakthrough—but then again there aren't actually many prophecies compared to the merchandising posts. They mostly post screenshots from PayPal of how much people are sowing into their ministry. I am shocked to see many of my friends in this group of 15,000. The influence may seem small, but these false prophets are either creating fake screenshots or they are bringing in $10,000 a week with their gimmicks.

The decision to go the way of Baal and or to go the way of Elijah lies in the prophet's heart. If pride, self-will, anger, or lust occupies the place where obedience, love, and truth should live, then the merchandising prophet may succeed in reaping worldly rewards for a season, but the retirement fund built on ill-gotten gains leads only to death (see Rom. 6:23). While there is certainly abundant grace for the true prophet who misses it, the Book of Revelation makes it clear that the false prophets (those who purposely set out to lie and deceive God's people) will be cast into the lake of fire and brimstone and be tormented day and night forever and ever (see Rev. 20:10).

## Don't Bow a Knee to Baal

> Prophets are a strange breed of men. They are God's emergency men for crisis hours. And the price of being a prophet is that a man has to live alone. All God's great men have been very, very lonely men.[1]

When I read words like this from Leonard Ravenhill, I'm challenged. When I look at the state of prophetic ministry today, I'm grieved.

Ravenhill was known for his no-comprising, hard-hitting, sin-blasting messages. He carried the spirit of a prophet. He carried a spirit like John the Baptist that laid the axe to the root—but he didn't do it with a critical, condemning heart. He did it with pure and undefiled love forged in the fire of God. Ravenhill once said:

The great need in America tonight, I'm convinced of this—as good as Bible schools are with their assembly lines and producing their preachers—the greatest need in America tonight is prophets. ...Ah, the prophets were men who walked with God, they felt like God, they saw like God, they wept like God, they yearned like God. They had no satisfaction....[2]

John the Baptist came doing no great miracles. As Ravenhill put it, "He didn't raise a dead man—he raised a dead nation." He lead the nation into the First Great Awakening—the coming of the Lord Jesus Christ. He was a forerunner, preparing the way of the Lord. And they chopped his head off.

Oh, I like to think of John Baptist standing there—no sponsors, nobody to agree or disagree with him. He stood there and they came to see this strange man anointed by the Holy Ghost.

...We have blinded our eyes to the truth and we have put our fingers in our ears to the voice of God. And the judgments are going to fall if we don't get revival, and maybe if it's not an alternative of Christ or chaos but Christ and chaos, not revival or revolution but revival and revolution; not revival without concentration camps; maybe the only place we'll get it is in concentration camps. Oh brother, we are heading for trouble, I'll tell you. Ah, the prophets were men who walked with God, they felt like God, they saw like God, they wept like God, they yearned like God.[3]

I know there are prophets like the ones Ravenhill described. I know there are thousands of prophets in the nation and around the world who have not bowed a knee to Baal. I know there are thousands who are not eating at Jezebel's table; thousands who are not selling personal prophecy on monthly installment plans; thousands who are nameless and faceless, with no public platform but a private prayer closet where God reveals to them His secrets. And they pray; they stand in the gap; they get in the watchtowers; they make up the hedge; they release intercession that touches heaven.

For all the haughty, arrogant, prideful prophets who believe they are called to rebuke major movements in the Body of Christ, there are many, many more who are weeping over the state of the nation. For all the doom-and-gloom prophets who release curses and leave no room for God's mercy, there are countless forerunners of awakening who are pointing to the next great move of God that will see a massive harvest come in.

For all the false prophets speaking smooth sayings for money, there are more who refuse to compromise the Word of God for ungodly gain. For all the Jezebel prophets leading the Church into false doctrines, there are many more who are calling the Church to repent in humility.

Lord, let the true prophets arise and glorify Your name, declare Your plans, and urge the Church to be salt and light in a lost and dying world!

## NOTE

1. Leonard Ravenhill, "The Spirit of a Prophet," https://www .youtube.com/watch?v=FE4bcpCCEuMandfeature=emb_title.

2. [[endnote needed]]

3. [[endnote needed]]

# CHAPTER 13

# SHARPENING YOUR DISCERNMENT

D iscernment. All Christians need it, but some haven't taken the time to cultivate it. There are two angles to explore—the gift of discerning of spirits and discernment. One is a gift. The other is developed. But even if you have the gift, you still need to cultivate it. The Bible is full of warnings about deception and cautions us to discern, and the pages of this book make it abundantly clear how urgent it is we sharpen our discernment.

If you've missed it, don't beat yourself up. If you've believed a false prophecy that took your life off track for a season, don't stop believing in the validity of prophetic ministry. Just commit to growing in discernment. Remember, anyone can miss it. Even anointed men of God in the Bible missed it badly and paid dear prices for their lack of discernment.

Joshua missed it. We read the following account in Joshua 9:1-16:

*And it came to pass when all the kings who were on this side of the Jordan, in the hills and in the lowland and in all the coasts of the Great Sea toward Lebanon— the Hittite, the Amorite, the Canaanite, the Perizzite, the Hivite, and the Jebusite—heard about it, that they gathered together to fight with Joshua and Israel with one accord.*

*But when the inhabitants of Gibeon heard what Joshua had done to Jericho and Ai, they worked craftily, and went and pretended to be ambassadors. And they took old sacks on their donkeys, old wineskins torn and mended, old and patched sandals on their feet, and old garments on themselves; and all the bread of their provision was dry and moldy. And they went to Joshua, to the camp at Gilgal, and said to him and to the men of Israel, "We have come from a far country; now therefore, make a covenant with us."*

*Then the men of Israel said to the Hivites, "Perhaps you dwell among us; so how can we make a covenant with you?" But they said to Joshua, "We are your servants." And Joshua said to them, "Who are you, and where do you come from?"*

*So they said to him: "From a very far country your servants have come, because of the name of the Lord your God; for we have heard of His fame, and all that He did in Egypt, and all that He did to the two kings of the Amorites who were beyond the Jordan—to Sihon king of Heshbon, and Og king of Bashan, who was at*

*Ashtaroth. Therefore our elders and all the inhabitants of our country spoke to us, saying, 'Take provisions with you for the journey, and go to meet them, and say to them, "We are your servants; now therefore, make a covenant with us."' This bread of ours we took hot for our provision from our houses on the day we departed to come to you. But now look, it is dry and moldy. And these wineskins which we filled were new, and see, they are torn; and these our garments and our sandals have become old because of the very long journey."*

*Then the men of Israel took some of their provisions; but they did not ask counsel of the Lord. So Joshua made peace with them, and made a covenant with them to let them live; and the rulers of the congregation swore to them. And it happened at the end of three days, after they had made a covenant with them, that they heard that they were their neighbors who dwelt near them.*

The Israelites later had to go to war to protect them because of the covenant.

## A Mighty Man of God Missed the Lie

Consider the account in First Kings 13:1-24:

*And behold, a man of God went from Judah to Bethel by the word of the Lord, and Jeroboam stood by the altar to burn incense. Then he cried out against the altar by the word of the Lord, and said, "O altar, altar! Thus says the Lord: 'Behold, a child, Josiah by name, shall be born to the house of David; and on you he shall sacrifice the priests of the high places who burn incense on you, and men's bones shall be burned on you.'" And he gave a sign the same day, saying, "This is the sign which the Lord has spoken: Surely the altar shall split apart, and the ashes on it shall be poured out."*

*So it came to pass when King Jeroboam heard the saying of the man of God, who cried out against the altar in Bethel, that he stretched out his hand from the altar, saying, "Arrest him!" Then his hand, which he stretched out toward him, withered, so that he could not pull it back to himself. The altar also was split apart, and the ashes poured out from the altar, according to the sign which the man of God had given by the word of the Lord. Then the king answered and said to the man of God, "Please entreat the favor of the Lord your God, and pray for me, that my hand may be restored to me."*

*So the man of God entreated the Lord, and the king's hand was restored to him, and became as before. Then the king said to the man of God, "Come home with me and refresh yourself, and I will give you a reward."*

*But the man of God said to the king, "If you were to give me half your house, I would not go in with you; nor would I eat bread nor drink water in this place. For so it was commanded me by the word of the Lord, saying, 'You shall not eat bread, nor drink water, nor return by the same way you came.'" So he went another way and did not return by the way he came to Bethel.*

*Now an old prophet dwelt in Bethel, and his sons came and told him all the works that the man of God had done that day in Bethel; they also told their father the words which he had spoken to the king. And their father said to them, "Which way did he go?" For his sons had seen which way the man of God went who came from Judah. Then he said to his sons, "Saddle the donkey for me." So they saddled the donkey for him; and he rode on it, and went after the man of God, and found him sitting under an oak. Then he said to him, "Are you the man of God who came from Judah?"*

*And he said, "I am." Then he said to him, "Come home with me and eat bread." And he said, "I cannot return with you nor go in with you; neither can I eat bread nor drink water with you in this place. For I have been told by the word of the Lord, 'You shall not eat bread nor drink water there, nor return by going the way you came.'"*

*He said to him, "I too am a prophet as you are, and an angel spoke to me by the word of the Lord, saying, 'Bring him back with you to your house, that he may eat bread and drink water.'" (He was lying to him.) So he went back with him, and ate bread in his house, and drank water.*

*Now it happened, as they sat at the table, that the word of the Lord came to the prophet who had brought him back; and he cried out to the man of God who came from Judah, saying, "Thus says the Lord: 'Because you have disobeyed the word of the Lord, and have not kept the commandment which the Lord your God commanded you, but you came back, ate bread, and drank water in the place of which the Lord said to you, "Eat no bread and drink no water," your corpse shall not come to the tomb of your fathers."'*

*So it was, after he had eaten bread and after he had drunk, that he saddled the donkey for him, the prophet whom he had brought back. When he was gone, a lion met him on the road and killed him. And his corpse was thrown on the road, and the donkey stood by it. The lion also stood by the corpse.*

## Samuel Missed the Heart of the Matter

Even Samuel missed it!

*So it was, when they came, that he looked at Eliab and said, "Surely the Lord's anointed is before Him!" But the Lord said to Samuel, "Do not look at his appearance or at his physical stature, because I have refused him. For the Lord does not see as man sees; for man looks at the outward appearance, but the Lord looks at the heart."*

*So Jesse called Abinadab, and made him pass before Samuel. And he said, "Neither has the Lord chosen this one." Then Jesse made Shammah pass by. And he said, "Neither has the Lord chosen this one." Thus Jesse made seven of his sons pass before Samuel. And Samuel said to Jesse, "The Lord has not chosen these." And Samuel said to Jesse, "Are all the young men here?" Then he said, "There remains yet the youngest, and there he is, keeping the sheep."*

*And Samuel said to Jesse, "Send and bring him. For we will not sit down till he comes here." So he sent and brought him in. Now he was ruddy, with bright eyes, and good-looking. And the Lord said, "Arise, anoint him; for this is the one!" Then Samuel took the horn of oil and anointed him in the midst of his brothers; and the Spirit of the Lord came upon David from that day forward. So Samuel arose and went to Ramah (1 Samuel 16:6-13).*

# What Discernment Is and How to Get It

Discernment is not a feeling. It's a knowing. If you have a feeling, don't act until the feeling is a knowing. Your emotions will betray your discernment. You need to see with your spirit and not your soul. Discernment over investment properties—one costs me, the other profits me. Discernment over friendships—one is strong, the other was a Jezebel. Discernment gets to the heart of the matter even if it doesn't make sense to our minds.

So how do we get discernment? First, desire discernment. First Corinthians 14:1 tells us to desire spiritual gifts. Discernment is one of the nine gifts of the Spirit. Second, ask God for discernment. James 1:5 tells us, "If any of you lacks wisdom, let him ask of God, who gives to all liberally and without reproach, and it will be given to him." Jesus invited us to: "Ask, and it will be given to you; seek, and you will find; knock, and it will be opened to you. For everyone who asks receives, and he who seeks finds, and to him who knocks it will be opened" (Matt. 7:7-8). Like wisdom, discernment flows out of a fear of the Lord. As we cultivate the fear of the Lord in our lives, we will gain discernment of what grieves Him.

Third, when you are not sure, seek godly counsel. I hear the voice of the Lord in good counsel. Our emotions can betray us. There are people who have more wisdom and discernment than you. You can sharpen your own skills by listening. Consider these two proverbs: "Where there is no counsel, the people fall; but in the multitude of counselors there is safety" (Prov. 11:14), and "Without counsel, plans go awry, but in the multitude of counselors they are established" (Prov. 15:22).

Fourth, be a student of the Word. The Word of God gives us God's perspective on all matters of life. The Book of Proverbs, in particular, is an excellent tool for strengthening your discernment. When we need discernment, we should pray and ask the Lord—then go to His Word. Judge your discernment against the Word of God. Hebrews 4:12 tells us, "For the word of God is living and powerful, and sharper than any two-edged sword, piercing even to the division of soul and spirit, and of joints and marrow, and is a discerner of the thoughts and intents of the heart," and Romans 12:2 pleas, "Do not be conformed to this world, but be transformed by the renewing of your mind, that you may prove what is that good and acceptable and perfect will of God."

Fifth, exercise discernment. In a warning of apostasy, the writer of Hebrews exhorts:

> *Concerning this we have much to say that is hard to explain, since you have become hard of hearing. For though by now you should be teachers, you need someone*

*to teach you again the first principles of the oracles of God and have come to need milk rather than solid food. Everyone who lives on milk is unskilled in the word of righteousness, for he is a baby. But solid food belongs to those who are mature, for those who through practice have powers of discernment that are trained to distinguish good from evil* (Hebrews 5:11-14 MEV).

And, finally, don't go by what you see with your natural eyes. John 7:24, "Do not judge according to appearance, but judge with righteous judgment."

Pray this prayer for discernment:

*Father, in the name of Jesus, I ask You to help me discern between good and evil, between the holy and the profane. Break any deception off my mind. Help me cast down any idols in my heart. Help me to judge a righteous judgment, without becoming critical and suspicious. Teach me to love what You love and hate what You hate. Teach me Your ways. Teach me Your Word. Make me more sensitive to Your Spirit so I will know when something is not Your will.*

# CONCLUSION

I had a troubling dream some years ago. It was a stark contrast between two prophets—one too busy to bear true kingdom fruit and the other too busy deceiving and being deceived.

The first prophet was a female. She was polite enough, but far too busy with far too many excuses about why she didn't have time for a quick visit. Ironically, she spent more time explaining why she didn't have time for a brief meeting than it would have taken to sit down and talk for a few minutes about how we could work together to bring more clarity to the prophetic movement.

I walked away feeling as if this prophet was full of pretense. She pretended to care about the people she was ministering to, but would never get close enough to allow them to see her for who she really was. She came off selfish and self-centered, self-important and self-absorbed. She had arrived and she wanted everyone to know it.

This prophet was more concerned about marketing than ministering, and if the meeting didn't advance her kingdom she wasn't interested in even taking the time to pray about what the Lord's will might be. I was disappointed because this prophet's public-facing ministry gave a much different impression than the face-to-face encounter I had just experienced.

## Little Shop of Horrors

When I turned around, I was in a Disney-like atmosphere, standing in a little bakery-type shop with goodies and coffees of many kinds. The smells were delightful. As I looked around, it was clear that I was in some sort of entertainment-oriented complex. But the little bakery I was in turned out to be more like a little shop of horrors.

A male prophet was running the establishment. Unlike the female prophet I had just encountered, this male prophet walked right over to me and engaged in friendly conversation. As soon as he began to speak, though, I discerned something was off. He was trying to impress me, to seduce me with his success. Soon enough, he began to prophesy over me. I didn't bear witness to what he was saying, but I politely listened to the prophetic puffery.

Suddenly, the prophetic word turned dark and frightful. His eyes glossed over as if he were staring into the distance. His lips stopped moving yet there were still words coming out of his mouth. It was his voice I heard, but it was coming from a short distance away. He was standing on the other side of the counter from me, but he was clearly no longer the one in control of his facilities. It was almost as if he were in some sort of trance—but it clearly wasn't from God. A slightly evil countenance was on his face.

I could feel the spirit of fear trying to grip me with false prophetic words about me slowly drowning in a lake inside a car. Not only was this prophetic word not coming from the Holy Spirit, it was purely demonic. I felt stuck there almost like I was glued to the floor, listening to this false prophet pontificate like the devil's ventriloquist. I could hear the words, but that was secondary to the discerning of spirits in motion. It was shocking.

Once this false prophet stopped spewing his fearful utterances, I figured he would want an offering for this deep revelation. I didn't have any money with me and I told him so. He waxed gracious and said he didn't do this for the money. That surprised me, as we so often associate false prophets with merchandising. But this false prophet wasn't in it for the money at all. He was motivated by something much more sinister. I'm still praying about what that motive is.

As I walked out of this bakery with all its cookies and cakes and coffees, I remember the temptation to turn around and enjoy some of the goodies. Instead, I walked out and called a young associate who shared with me a revelation she just received. She told me, excitedly, "No weapon formed against me can prosper!"

I took the experience I had just walked through with the two prophets as a teaching tool and began to share what had just happened. Now I am sharing it with you. I am not one to get goofy over dreams and visions. But this one was so real and stayed with me when I woke up. I couldn't shake it. I knew I had to record it and seek the Lord for its meaning, then share it with others, both those who are just learning to sharpen their discernment and those who have been around the circuits.

# Scripture Parallels

I hesitate to interpret something just for the sake of offering an interpretation. But I can tell you what Jesus said, and I believe these two Scriptures describe these two prophets.

Regarding the female prophet, I sense to apply this Scripture:

> *Beware of false prophets, who come to you in sheep's clothing, but inwardly they are ravenous wolves. You will know them by their fruits. Do men gather grapes from thornbushes or figs from thistles? Even so, every good tree bears good fruit, but a bad tree bears bad fruit. A good tree cannot bear bad fruit, nor can a bad tree bear good fruit. Every tree that does not bear good fruit is cut down and thrown into the fire. Therefore by their fruits you will know them.*

> *Not everyone who says to Me, "Lord, Lord," shall enter the kingdom of heaven, but he who does the will of My Father in heaven. Many will say to Me in that day, "Lord, Lord, have we not prophesied in Your name, cast out demons in Your name, and done many wonders in Your name?" And then I will declare to them, "I never knew you; depart from Me, you who practice lawlessness!"* (Matthew 7:15-23)

And regarding the male prophet, I sense to apply this Scripture:

> *Then if anyone says to you, "Look, here is the Christ!" or "There!" do not believe it. For false christs and false prophets will rise and show great signs and wonders to*

*deceive, if possible, even the elect. See, I have told you beforehand* (Matthew 24:23-25).

One thing is certain, false prophets are rising in this hour. The Bible warns of false prophets over and over again and I am quickened in my spirit to sound the alarm.

Look beyond the outside of the vessel and discern the spirit operating in the background. I'm not suggesting going on a witch hunt. I'm just pleading with you to take heed to the Bible's warning not to be deceived—and don't think you can't be.

Work out your salvation with fear and trembling. Stay grounded in the Word of God. Seek Him rather than supernatural experiences. Walk in love and be quick to forgive. False prophets are rising. And they look like sheep. Exercise discernment.

# ABOUT
# JENNIFER LECLAIRE

Jennifer is senior leader of Awakening House of Prayer in Fort Lauderdale, Florida, founder of the Ignite Network, and founder of the Awakening Blaze prayer movement. Jennifer formerly served as the first-ever female editor of *Charisma* magazine and is a prolific author of over 25 books. You can find Jennifer online or shoot her an email at info@jenniferleclaire.org.